Philosophy, Human Life and Society

About the Author

Sanchita Bora, born in 1973 in a village at Missamora, Assam completed her early education in Missamora Higher Secondary School and Dergaon Kamal Duwera College. She completed her M. A. (Philosophy) from Gauhati University in 1996. She was awarded Ph.D. by Gauhati University in 2012 on "The Philosophy of Value: An Evaluation of Indian Perspectives" under the guidance of Prof. Girish Sharma.

Though poetry is her first love, she is also a prolific writer of philosophical essays in both Assamese and English. She published a book of Assamese poems in 2012. She has written more than 20 articles on different philosophical thoughts, especially on value philosophy, and published in *The Assam Tribune, Sutradhar, Goriyoshi* etc. To her credit, there are more than 40 research papers published in peer reviewed journals, conference proceedings and presented in national and international seminars. She also contributed many book chapters in books published by different organisations.

Presently, she teaches Philosophy in Nowgong Girls' College, Nagaon, Assam.

PHILOSOPHY, HUMAN LIFE AND SOCIETY

Value Perspectives

Sanchita Bora

CONCEPT PUBLISHING COMPANY PVT. LTD.
NEW DELHI-110059

ISBN-13: 978-93-86682-41-3

First Published 2018

Published and Printed by:

Concept Since 1974

Concept Publishing Company Pvt. Ltd.
A/15-16, Commercial Block, Mohan Garden,
New Delhi-110059 (INDIA)
T : +91 11 25351460, +91 11 25351794
E-publishing@conceptpub.com, *W* : www.conceptpub.com

Cataloging in Publication Data--Courtesy: D.K. Agencies (P) Ltd. <docinfo@dkagencies.com>

Bora, Sanchita, 1973- **author.**
Philosophy, human life and society : value perspectives / Sanchita Bora.
pages cm
Includes bibliographical references and index.
ISBN 9789386682413

1. Life. 2. Values—India. 3. Social problems—India. 4. Social sciences—India—Philosophy. 5. Philosophy, Indic. I. Title.

LCC BD431.B67 2018 DDC 128 23

Dedicated to my Parents

Preface

Philosophy asks the basic questions and problems faced by human beings. These questions are related to Metaphysics, Epistemology and Axiology. Metaphysics asks 'what is reality', 'what is being'. Epistemology enquires 'what is knowledge', 'how do we know'. And Axiology questions 'what is value'? But, philosophy is not simply a theory; it is a way of life. Though philosophy is part of a curriculum of studies, it has enormous influence on our everyday lives. Every institution of society is based on philosophical ideas. Philosophy is about the intelligent and rational uses of knowledge. In many cases it is about deciding which goals and values are worthy to pursue. Philosophy is an activity, a pursuit, a form of thinking meant to guide human growth in society. So, there is a close relation between society and value. We know that to an isolated man morality is meaningless. The significance of human life is determined by the presence and experience of social aspirations. Therefore, philosophical outlook of a human being is determined by the integration and harmonization of social and personal aspects.

Human values find manifestation in the context of interaction among human beings in society. Present society is confronted with critical problems which raise value perspectives. Again, value situation creates social consequences. So, it should be our duty to create a value climate which will encourage goodness in human being and in society. One's life ought to be lived in such a way that nobody feels injured by his or her lifestyle, deed and talks.

I have a keen interest in the value system of society. Guiding by this concern, I have written different articles on social issues and value perspectives. This work is a humble attempt to give them a book form. It is a collection of seventeen chapters which simply observes human life and different issues of society in terms of value. The first chapter confirms that every normally developed person is in some degree a philosopher. The life of an individual is elevated by the philosophical outlook and such outlook has metaphysical, psychological, ethical and religious comportments. The next three chapters (*Society, Individual and Value, Social Integration and Value: An Overview of Ancient Indian Thought, Social Changes and Value Standpoint*) demonstrate how value sense makes man unique. These chapters illustrate the importance of value in different contexts of social life. The chapter *Value Inculcation through Folk Tales* proclaims that folk tales are the effective tools to educate a child. They can implant divine values and a deep sense of humanism in tender mind of a child.

The chapter *Dharma and Present day Society* shows metaphysical and axiological significance of the concept *Dharma*. It affirms that all our present day problems are the results of disregarding *Dharma*. This piece of writing demonstrates the role of *Dharma* in current social problems. Another chapter *Eco-Feminism: A Brief Outline* presents really a brief outline of Eco-Feminism as a social movement. Eco-Feminism offers a potentially transformative philosophy of the self and society. Basic Eco-Feminist position introduces social and ecological issues and rouse value stance.

Revisiting Family Values is the chapter in which it is clearly mentioned that once people begin to show respect for family values our society will be a better place to live without any fear of insecurity. Again, *Indian Value System: Its relevance in 21st Century* is the chapter which tries to establish that the age-old scheme of *Puruṣārtha* is organically related to human nature. Even in 21st century, the four *Puruṣārthas* need to be held together in a balanced interdependent way to maintain harmony in both individual and social life. A truthful interplay of traditional and modern values is the need of this hour.

The chapter *Conflict, Conflict Resolution and National Integration* says that different people with different goals and needs come into conflicts frequently. But, we should not let the conflict to control us. Diplomacy, negotiation, co-existence and peace building are instrumental to conflict resolution and the concept national integration itself stimulates a value climate. *Education and Dimensions of Human Personality* states that education is for all-round development of the many dimensional human personality. But, at present technological progress introduces deeper social, psychological and cultural issues. So, effective education should enable the individual to fit them in new value situations of the changing environment.

The chapter *Women Empowerment: Issues regarding Power and Powerlessness* introduces the most discussed ideal of women emancipation. Social, economic and political factors put women as inferior to men. But, 'proper education' is only the approach to replace inhuman values by human values. To strike a balance between power and powerlessness situation, we have to cope with ever-changing value situation. Another chapter *Cultural Globalization: An Observation of Indian Scenario* categorically declares that cultural globalization provides better understanding of values and attitudes of different communities across the globe. It has both merits and demerits on current Indian society. But, one has to understand social complexity and value change to explore a good life.

Two chapters are included on the two prominent concepts of M.K. Gandhi and Dr. S. Radhakrishnan as both the thinkers have great influence on Contemporary Indian philosophy. Non-violent state is the ideal for Gandhi and *sarvamukti* is the ideal for Radhakrishnan. Both ideals can never be realized fully. But, these ideals represent living thoughts and advocate that striving after the ideal is essential for rebuilding of society.

Last two chapters are on two sovereign personalities of Assam — Sri Śaṅkaradeva and Dr. Bhupen Hazarika's living social thoughts. Sri Śaṅkaradeva (1449-1568), the great medieval *Vaiṣṇava* saint of Assam had reconstructed Assamese society and culture. He had brought dual revolution — revolution in the minds of man and revolution in the structure of society. On the other hand, in present era, *Asam Ratna* Dr. Bhupen Hazarika (1926-2011), an artist of multi-faceted talents revolutionized the society by his evergreen songs. He wrote his first song (1937) in which he acknowledged the priceless contribution of Sri Śaṅkaradeva. Sri Śaṅkaradeva considered social reconstruction in terms of self-purification. Again, the prime subjects of Dr. Bhupen Hazarika's songs are love, humanism and social uplift. Both tried to instil fellow feeling and love in the hearts of man and dreamt of a classless society.

Hope these chapters will instil inquisition in the minds of readers and open up new vistas of philosophical outlook towards social values for making the society more harmonious and rational.

Nagaon (Assam)

Sanchita Bora
e-mail: sanchita.bora@gmail.com

Acknowledgements

It is really difficult to specify only few persons who contributed directly or indirectly in this endeavour. Every person, friend or foe, well-wisher or detractor has always enriched me through the journey of inquisition. I try to relate philosophical thought to the life of human being. I strongly believe that philosophy should be studied by keeping the human life and society as the pivot.

My parents Sri Khogeswar Bora and Smt. Suraprabha Bora and my mother-in-law Smt. Subhadra Bora have been my great educator and inspiration. Though I love playing with words for my poetry, I perhaps cannot compose any sentence to thank them, whatever I say that may belittle their contribution for making me what I am.

I have been fortunate to meet few very good teachers in my academic pursuit who have opened the windows for me to the beautiful world of wisdom. I am dwarf in front of them, but they also taught me to touch the sky. I record my sincere gratitude to all my teachers of DKD College and Gauhati University.

Knowledge should be transmitted, discussed and debated. This should also be kept in organised way for the posterity. The repeated insistence of my husband Prof. Pradip Bora made me thinking to compile the articles in book form. I do not know how much successful I am as a mother, but my daughter Sapontara's inquisitive face and her innocence always remind me my duty as a teacher. I see her face in every girl that I teach in my college. I cannot thank them, because I am in them and they are in me.

I should thank our family friend Mr. Sashi Kumar of Scientific Book Centre for his personal interest and help in this endeavour. I also thank Mr. Ashok Kumar Mittal, Managing Director and

Mr. Nitin Mittal of Concept Publishing Company (P) Ltd., New Delhi for their support in publishing this book.

Place: Guwahati **Sanchita Bora**
Date: 25th December, 2017

Contents

Section III
Reflections on Living Thoughts

Section I

Human Life, Society and Value

1
Human Life, Philosophy and Philosophical Outlook

Man, being rational can consider how best he can live. Reflection is the basic character of man. Life is a fact and we naturally ask questions: What is life? What is its value and destiny? What is the proper place of man in the democracy of things? With an unusually strenuous effort to seek an answer to these momentous questions we all become philosophers in non-academic sense. What a person wants to get and what he wants to give will depend on his own philosophy of life. It is common that each person bears a philosophical system in his thought, because it is absurd to think of a rational being without philosophical outlook. Every normally developed person, if he lives reflectively, is in some degree a philosopher.

Perry says, "Philosophy is neither accidental nor supernatural but inevitable and normal."[1] The word 'Philosophy' has a beautiful practical exercise. It is an active theory, a conclusive way to conduct our life. If we are not using any adjective, like political, economical, educational etc. in front of the word Philosophy, it simply means philosophy of life. The root of philosophy is the reflection upon life and the world. "Man and his values are primary; their primacy has to be acknowledged by any philosophy."[2] There is a common conception of philosophy that it is impractical, without any significance or utility. A little but minute observation will prove that it is a misconception. Actually, philosophy springs directly from man's life and its needs. True philosophy is nothing but a general theory of human life and its environment.

Every human being has a duty to preserve and to promote life. So, he has at least a dogmatic and superficial philosophy of life based upon his temperament according to which he moulds his activities. There is no choice between philosophy and no philosophy. Philosophy is the rational attempt to have a world-view. It endeavors to reach a conception of the entire universe with all its elements and aspects and their interrelations to one another. Philosophy is the criticism or interpretation of life. At this moment, it is regarded more as an interpretation of human life, its source, value, meaning and destiny than as an enquiry into the nature of the world, soul and God. It tries to understand the universe in relation to man. It seeks to give a rational conception of the reality as a whole, which satisfies man's deepest intellectual, moral, aesthetic and religious aspirations.

Philosophy is considered to be the ultimate enquiry about life and its existence. It is a pursuit of knowledge dealing with the principles, causes and laws regarding life, human nature, creation, principles of living and the conduct of human activity. Reflective thought is man's peculiar power. Real progress of the human race which the world is observing in every field has come through the medium of reflective thinking. If such reflective thinking becomes serious, sustained and logical it will be 'philosophy'. Then only it is engaged to answer the questions of life and values. Philosophy is the essential occupation of human life. Life and philosophy react upon each other. Thoreau said that to be a philosopher is not merely to have subtle thoughts, nor even to found a school, but so to love wisdom as to live, according to its dictates, a life of simplicity, independence, magnanimity and trust.

One's philosophy of life is connected to one's world-view. Again, the connotation of the term 'outlook' suggests the synthesis of beliefs and attitudes. "Outlook is the life's implicit spiritual basis and assumption: life is its explicit form and expression."[3] The outlook, to be philosophical, must express one's synoptic thought about world and life. A person can realize his concrete existence when he is able to develop a philosophical outlook. Sometimes, philosophical outlook has been confused and identified with other worldliness, asceticism, mysticism, theism etc. Therefore, we must be clear about the positive configurations and contents of the philosophical outlook in life. We find that this outlook consists of four constituents: (1) metaphysical, (2) psychological, (3) ethical and (4) religious.

The metaphysical foundation lies in the individual's deliberate views, beliefs and attitudes, regarding the nature of the universe and the place of human life in it. The main metaphysical questions are: Is the universe a mechanical interplay of material atoms? Or, is it the manifestation of some kind of purpose? Is the universe the manifestation of dead physico-chemical processes, or the operation of a spirit? Is there nothing but matter and energy? What is life? What is death? What is Self ? What is consciousness? etc. Every human being tries to fit suitable answers to all these questions. It proves that an individual is not the result of dead mechanism.

The second constituent of the philosophical outlook is the psychological basis of life. Psychology is the study of mind and of behaviour as the expression of mind. Life must have a psychological basis in the form of belief, attitudes regarding the nature and functions of the mind that, directly or indirectly, shapes all human life and behaviour. What is mind? What is its nature? And what is the practical bearing of all these on the conduct of human life? Every human being living meaningfully in the society tries to answer all these questions in his own way. It is the "realization of the motivated character of the mind; and cultivation of a conscientious habit of truthful self-exploration of motives with a view to integration and harmonization of personality."[4]

The third ingredient of the philosophical outlook is the ethical orientation of life. If life must have a metaphysical foundation and a psychological basis, it must further, also have an ethical orientation. This ethical foundation consists of appropriate beliefs and attitudes regarding the ultimate goal of human life. It is also about the nature and modes of life conducive to that goal. The study of ultimate goal of all our life's aspiration has occupied the human mind from the dawn of reflection. What a man ought to be or do naturally depends on what man is. The nature of ethical goal of human life can only be ascertained after having due regard to the nature of human existence (metaphysical foundation) and human nature (psychological foundation). Ethics determines the art and goals of good living.

Finally, there remains the religious coping. If man's life must have a metaphysical foundation, a psychological basis and an ethical orientation, it must have also the finishing touch and grace of a religious coping. It is the appropriate beliefs and attitudes regarding the nature of the ultimate ground and sanction of the moral obligations that devolve in his life. Morality and religion are closely connected with each other. Religious experience is as old as smiling and weeping, loving and forgiving. It is concerned with the elevation of human personality. Love for humanity and devotion are the genuine expressions of true religion. Religion springs from the spiritual constitution of man and we know that man is a composite being having mental, physical and spiritual aspects. This fourth constituent of philosophical outlook signifies that an individual has obligations not only for the society but also for the whole universe.

"Man is the common denominator with reference to which religions, philosophies, political and social ideologies and even science are tested."[5] The common element that is associated with the above three—life, philosophy and philosophical outlook—is the nature of human being. There are never ending controversies regarding man's nature. But it is clear that the change and development of an individual are physical, social as well as cultural. As he lives in a physical and social environment, he, at any rate cannot ignore others' individuality. With respect to the curiosity whether human life has any meaning, W.H. Halverson has mentioned the theory of cosmic purpose. "Everything that occurs in the world is part of a grand design, and that every individual human life derives its highest meaning from its participation in the whole."[6] That's why the guiding force of each and every plan of individual life should be the philosophical outlook. To live as a real member of human society is one's duty and responsibility also.

Notes

1. Perry, R.B., 2013. *The Approach to Philosophy.* Start Publishing LLC eBook edition, p. 10.
2. Patrick, G.T.W. & Chapman, F.M., 1961. *Introduction to Philosophy,* George Allen & Unwin Ltd., p. 8.
3. Halverson, W.H., 1976. *A Concise Introduction to Philosophy.* New York: Random House, p. 416.
4. Schweitzer, A., 1933. *Out of My Life and Thought.* New York and Toronto: Mentor Books, p. 126 as quoted in *A Concise Introduction to Philosophy,* W.H. Halverson (1976), New York: Random House, p. 413.
5. Radhakrishnan, S. & Raju, P.T. (ed.), 1995. *The Concept of Man* (*A Study in Comparative Philosophy*). New Delhi: Indus, p. 16.
6. *Ibid.*, p. 23.

2
Society, Individual and Value

Franz Oppenheimer expresses the view that society is the totality of concepts of all purely natural relations and institutions between man and man. The individuality of a person needs society for its ample manifestation and development. Society has become a biological necessity for man. Man is also psychologically equipped to live in society. R.K. Mukherjee writes "Man is a unique creature in the evolutionary process and society a distinctive achievement."[1] Man's emotional development, his intellectual maturity and even his material comforts cannot be thought of without society. Man has certain innate urges in common with the lower animals. But, man combines in his nature not merely instinctive urges of the animal life but also a higher spiritual principle. His native capacity of conscious reflection and inner determination, when directed towards certain ends like sex-desires and food, can divest them of their animal character and transform them into pursuits worthy of human nature.

The very qualifying word *human* in human pursuit or human end suggests that it does not mean those ends or objects which both man and lower animals seek in common. Human beings have higher aims than mere physical survival. Because of the human aspect of man, as put by Mackenzie man refuses to be guided by instinct alone. Only man consciously reflects upon right and wrong behaviour, approving or disapproving. Valuation is a part of man's social living. The human child gets the lesson of conduct first from parents and then from society. Out of the give and take between man and society, the good life springs. Aristotle's view is that society is for the sake of good life. Durkheim also puts forward the thesis that society is a dynamic system and the seat of moral life.

Every man faces the challenge of Good and Pleasant. It is the value-sense which distinguishes man from the other animals and makes him unique. All values refer to the human self as the agent and the enjoyer. Some represent the needs of our emotional, impulsive self, while some others reflect self-determination. Values live in and through man and his life. Human life is purposive and it implies ideals and values sought by him. Values are goals set for achievements and they motivate, define and colour all our activities. Values symbolize the generally accepted and acceptable codes of human behaviour, certain principles and standards which guide and influence the conduct of individuals and ultimately of the community. Sometimes, values are described as the socially defined designs and goals that are internalized through the process of conditioning, learning and socialization. Values are standards and patterns of choice that guide persons and groups towards satisfaction, fulfilment and meaning. Earlier the word 'value' was used only as a verb meaning to value or esteem something or as a singular noun, meaning the measure of a thing, for example, the economic value of money, labour or property. But value also means the moral beliefs and attitudes of a society.

The relationship between individual and society is the most profound problems of social philosophy. It involves the question of values. Society is a group of individuals in reciprocal interaction that is value. The individual is the active agent of culture. In society, values are ideals that guide or qualify one's (individual's) personal conduct and interaction with others. Values serve as channels of communication and rational discussion between members of a society. Values help individuals to distinguish what is right and what is wrong and inform him on how he can conduct his life in a meaningful way.

An individual is surrounded and encompassed by culture and societal force. E. Durkheim rightly says, "The core of the social system, its very soul, is the system of ideals of value."[2] Therefore, the individual has to conform to the norms of the society. Apparently, values within society can be classified into four categories: Personal Values, Cultural Values, Social Values and Work Values. Personal values are principles that define the member of society as an individual. Personal values, such as honesty, reliability, and trust, determine how an individual will face the world and relate with people. Cultural values, like the practice of one's faith and customs, are principles that sustain connections with his cultural roots. They help the individual feel connected to a larger community of people with similar backgrounds. Social values are principles that indicate how an individual relates meaningfully to others in social situations; including those involving family, friends, and co-workers. Work values are principles that guide one's behaviour in professional contexts. They define how an individual works and how he relates to his co-workers, bosses, and clients. These principles reveal individual's potential for advancement.

The moral worth of a society is reflected on the values it cherishes, the ideals it pursues and its sincerity in upholding them. Values reflect both the actual state of society and its aspirations. Values serve as the authorities in the name of which choices are made and actions are taken. Values may be either preferences or principles. If values are preferences, they are personal choices and subjective. On the other hand, if they are principles, they are consistent, universal and objective. Individual sense of values is communicated from person to person through society and its institutions. Man expresses value-judgement and choice in respect of desirability and undesirability, truth and falsehood, beauty and ugliness, rightness and wrongness of behaviour. Life in society is the backdrop against which alone man can hope to actualize his aspiration for values.

Society is for awaking the creative and other potentialities of the members. The progress of society is such an evolution which satisfies a rational criterion of value. The attainment of common good is the essence of the ideal society and here lies the significance of moral and spiritual elements of the individual. The moral progression of men in society is the pre-condition of their social progress. Herd sentiment of society maintains whole system of morality; embodies approval and disapproval (of the herd) and inspires recognition.

We may consider human society-value-individual as a triangle. Society imbibes values in each individual. In return individuals' acts and behaviour reflect social ethics and cultural ethos. Sociality is always present in each individual. Again, society is also an integral part of the individuality. The "quality of life" or the "standard of life" is determined by the eternal values of man and society. They must be regarded as interdependent processes in a whole configuration.

The end of all moral action is a social order in which each member of the group may have a fair field for his activities and the fullest opportunity for self-development, without infringing upon the similar right of every other member of the group in the present or in future generations. Though the individuality of a man is the combination of three aspects body, mind and soul, he is interconnected with his fellowmen. If someone strives for perfection one has to shed his egoistic desires and anti-social tendencies. It is true that a civilized society or a cultured nation can continue its existence with a positive attitude towards moral and social values. Value is of such a nature that any outlook of life and the universe involves some phase of it. Values are conceived with reference to the need of the harmonious functioning of the society.

Notes

1. Mukerjee, R.K., 1950. *The Dynamics of Morals: A Socio-psychological Theory of Ethics,* p. 86.
2. Durkheim, E., 1965. *Sociology and Philosophy.* Translated by Pockock, p. xxiv.

3
Social Integration and Value: An Overview of Ancient Indian Thought

Society is an organized group of individuals who interacting with one another form a cohesive unit. It is described as a web of relationships and it is an ever-changing complex system. S. Gopalan writes, "….. society liberates and limits the activities of man, sets up standards for them to follow and maintain; whatever the imperfections and tyrannies it has exhibited in human history, it is necessary condition of every fulfilment of life."[1]

Social integration is complex and touchy idea. It generally implies the tendency of a society to preserve its integrity as a social group. The basic aim of social integration is to create a "society for all". In an integrated society each member has an active role to play with both rights and responsibilities. Social integration, in other words is the process of linking individuals through the use of such activities which enable communication, development and skills necessary to function in a given society. Social integration also involves social stability and permanence.

Though social integration means different things to different people, three different ways of understanding this concept are formulated—

(i) An inclusionary or positive goal, implying equal opportunities and rights for all human beings.

(ii) Conjuring up the image of an unwanted imposition of conformity.

(iii) A way of describing the established patterns of human relations in any given society.

Social integration reflects and promotes harmonious interaction and solidarity at all levels of society. Durkheim believed strongly in the importance of social integration. He theorized that integration gives humankind purpose and meaning in life. Lack of social integration leads to what Durkheim saw as a dangerous state of mind.

Indian philosophy of value has definite social implications. Values are based on a consideration of one's fellow beings living in the society. Indian philosophy concerns with the welfare of the human race which it regards as one family. It repeatedly makes clear exposition of welfare of the society (*lokasaṁgraha* and *lokakalyāṇa*). "From the *Brāhmaṇas* onwards, through the *Sūtras* literature down to the *Smṛtis*, we find that the tendency towards the external observance of rituals has been joined up with the notion of social good as well."[2]

The division of duty is neatly prescribed by Indian tradition. There are two main types of duties—*Sādhāraṇa Dharma* or general duties and *Viśeṣa Dharma* or specific duties. The *Sādhāraṇa Dharma* are virtues like *Dhṛti* or fortitude, *Kṣamā* or forbearance, *Dama* or control over mind, *Asteya* or earning money by rightful means or strict adherence to one's own possessions without desire to take other's, *Śauca* or purity in thought, word and deed, *Indriyanigraha* or control over sense organs, *Dhī* or clarified understanding or intellect, *Vidyā* or knowledge of truth or education, *Satya* or truthfulness, *Akrodha* or freedom from anger etc. and these should be practiced by all, irrespective of their age, sex, social status etc. The other type of duty was specific for every individual. Society was divided into the four *Varṇas* and their duty is to strictly conform to the nature. Each *Varṇa* has specific duties. Yet again, there are four stages or *Āśramas* through which every individual has to pass his life. These *Āśramas* have also set of well-defined duties. "According to the dominant social philosophy of traditional India, society should be organized into classes of individuals, each class making its peculiar contribution to the well-being of society, and the life of the individual should be divided into various stages, so that each person might make the maximum contribution to the well-being of society at the same time contribute maximally to his or her own self-perfection."[3]

Again, *Puruṣārtha* is the collective name for the four aspirations (viz., *Dharma, Artha, Kāma* and *Mokṣa*) of human life which constitute the scheme of value. Though *Kāma* means any desire or pleasure, it does not refer to purely selfish pleasure which is enjoyed at the cost of others. *Kāma* is not just any desire giving rise to any pleasure; it is the desire which man seeks in his social relationship with others. Same is the case with *Artha*. It can never be an object of desire in the scheme of valuation if it promotes an egoistic sense. When a *Puruṣa* or individual is well aware of himself as a member of society then only he can transform wealth to a value or *Puruṣārtha*. *Dharma* points to duty and it also supplies a rationale or justification for duties. The strict observance of one's *Dharma* in a spirit of detachment guarantees individual and social welfare. *Dharma* is both the process and the instrument of integration. *Mokṣa* indicates the concept of spiritual perfection. *Mokṣa* implies that the highest truth is the self and the good consists in its realization of what it is in its original integrity.

Society is constituted of individuals and its primary object is to safeguard and promote the interest of the individual. It is frequently observed that interest of the society and the individual be at odds with each other. Individuals differ in natural aptitudes. They have also differences in their respective disposition (*svadharma*). And these differences carry the division of labour in society for mutual co-existence. M.D. Chaturvedi observed that the *Āśramas* and the *Varṇas* were defined in order to show people, what kind of virtues they should aim at in a particular place or time in which they find themselves and help their orderly evolution. "Each *Varṇa* is designed to occupy a particular position in the society, not with reference to any advantage or special rights but with reference to its capability....certain types of work are considered as belonging to certain groups. The *Varṇadharma* denies accumulation of wealth for ones' own use only."[4]

Ancient Indian scriptures help in maintaining an orderly society, the family, the village, the region and the country. The stability and orderly development of society and the happiness of the individuals is dependent on the rulers fulfilling their duties and responsibilities. *Rājadharma* deals with rights, privileges and responsibilities of the rulers and it is an important subject of *Dharmaśāstra* and *Arthaśāstra*.

Originally, there was nothing inherently wrong in the scheme of *Varṇa* system. It points out that all work is socially useful and equally important. So, no class is less essential. On the basis of this system, the faculties, the talents, aptitudes and skills were perpetually promoted. But, in due course of time, the real purpose of the class system was hampered mainly due to economic exploitation of one class on other. Moreover, when foreign invaders and rulers came to India they wanted to serve their purpose by causing conflicts among different classes.

Social integration is made one of the three priority areas for action identified at the World Summit for Social Development held in Copenhagen in 1995. Social integration is recognized as a dominant objective of social and economic development. At present, call for social integration is growing. The dishonest tendency of different institutions and organizations of society reflects decline of civility and tolerance in day-to-day social relations. As a result, criminal activities and corruption are increasing. Even sometimes young people are abandoned or brutalized. In the society values are ideals that guide or qualify one's (individual's) personal conduct and interaction with others. The social process involves the relationship among social choice, human conduct and progress. This relationship requires values for a meaningful interaction.

Notes

1. Gopalan, S., *Hindu Social Philosophy*, p. 6.
2. Dasgupta, S., *Development of Moral Philosophy in India*, p. 14.
3. Koller, J.M., *Puruṣārthas as Human Aims*, p. 315.
4. Grover, U., *Varṇa Dharma* or Caste System. In S. Narang (ed.), *Dharmaśāstra in Contemporary Times*, p. 117.

4
Social Changes and Value Standpoint

To be human is to be social. Generally, society is used to mean the totality of human relations. An individual cannot achieve what he wants to be outside any society. 'Society' is about how people organize and conduct their lives. On the other hand, change is the law of life. It is inevitable in social reality; a central feature of human social existence. People's ideas, acts and behaviour and cultures have been witnessing remarkable transformation due to social changes."[1]

Values are rooted in human life and society. They are to be embodied and experienced in social activities, relationships and institutions. Values are derived from the social environment in which we live and work. Today, innovative spirit of human has made the world small by unifying it in varieties of ways. At this juncture, conflict of values is a common happening. Misconceived notions of modernity have caused a great threat to our age old values. But, it is also mention worthy that new setting and new contents of values are arising. Values are important for social equilibrium. They are the keys for better understanding of social changes.

Men do not stop with a factual view of their experience. Explicitly or implicitly they are persistently regarding things as good or bad, as true or false as virtues or vices. Values serve as criteria for selection in action, judgement, preference and choice. "We cannot think that objects of the world, persons, events and actions are value-free. Value is a logically prior concept, and as such incapable of definition."[2]

What may be the exact meaning of value; it is a source of much misunderstanding. But nobody can deny that value is the very framework of the world. Most commonly, values are the basis upon which an individual will choose one course rather than another, judged as better or worse, right or wrong. They symbolize the generally accepted and acceptable code of human behaviour, certain principles and standards which guide and influence the conduct of individuals and ultimately of the community. We all know that values are goals set for achievements and they motivate, define and colour all our activities. Values are the desirable end states. They act as a guide to human endeavour.

Social Changes

Heraclitus is the earliest and best known ancient Greek philosopher who emphasized the primacy of change. "Change is such an evident feature of social reality that any social scientific theory whatever its conceptual starting point must sooner or later address it."[3] Change is a central feature of human social existence. Social change is a very basic term. It remains central question for all classical founders of sociology. Issues of change and stability have been occupying the minds of great social thinkers since earlier times. Auguste Comte, the father of sociology has divided his system of theory into two separate parts: social statics and social dynamics. To Comte, the study of social statics, that is, of the conditions and preconditions of social order, was inevitably linked to the study of social dynamics, which he equated with human progress and evolution. Social static focuses on how order is maintained in the society and social dynamic focuses on how society changes over time.

Social change is a twig of sociology, but it involves political science, economics, history, anthropology and many other social sciences. Social change refers to an alteration in the structure, a change in the nature of social institutions, social behaviours and social relations of a society. In other words, social change is the transformation of culture and social organization and structure over time which may be driven by cultural, religious, economic, scientific or technological forces. It may refer to the notion of social progress or socio-cultural evolution; to a paradigmatic change in the socio-economic structure, and also to social revolution.

"The basic concept of social change involves three ideas: 1. difference, 2. at the different temporal moments, and 3. between states of the same system."[4] We are aware that society is never static, social, political, economic and cultural changes occur constantly.

Social change in the broadest sense is any change in social relations. It is an ever-present phenomenon in any society. But "the subject was born in the nineteenth century as an attempt to comprehend the fundamental transition from traditional to modern society, the rise of the urban, industrial, capitalist order."[5]

"The most striking feature of contemporary life is the revolutionary pace of social change. Never before have things changed so fast for so much of mankind. Everything is affected: art, science, religion, morality, education, politics, the economy, family life, even the inner aspect of our lives – nothing has escaped" (Lenski and Lenski, 1974:3).[6] The main causes of social change are the cultural, technological, biological, demographical, environmental, and psychological and so on.

We are not going to cite the list of specific changes those have been taking place in our society and also their sources or origination. Even to the casual eye, we are able to notice innumerable changes in our society. An important feature of social change is that each and every change is open to be considered as positive as well as negative, constructive as well as destructive, optimistic as well as pessimistic.

Social Change and Value

Social change is a structural transformation of political, social and economic systems and institutions to create a more equitable and just society and it is a universal phenomenon and it occurs in every society. Technically said that social change refers to an alteration in the social order of a social group or society; a change in the nature, social institutions, social behaviours or social relations of a society. As we know change is inevitable and it takes place in all fields. The term 'social change' is often used to describe variations or modifications of any respect of social process, social patterns, social interaction or social organization.

Again, values are rooted in human historicity. They are to be experienced and created by the individual. They are embodied in social activities, relationships and institutions. Social values are principles that indicate how one relates meaningfully to others in social situations, including those involving family, friends, and co-workers. Values reside in the situation, in the field in which an individual participates. Our values are derived from the social environment in which we live and work. Value formation takes place under the impact of current societal and institutional demands. In this way they are important for understanding various changing socio-psychological phenomena.

Today man's innovative spirit has made the world small by unifying it in varieties of ways. The new global transformation has lent a distinctive existence to man. He has been assured material well being in all spheres. The most prominent character of contemporary life is the revolutionary haste of social change. Man's perception of the world, as well as his attitudes towards life has also been changed. Deep-rooted changes in mass worldwide are reshaping economic, political and social life. Now, we live in a new age of science and technology. At the age of super-growth of industry and technology, we cannot discard technical knowledge. But technological progress very often introduces wider and deeper social, psychological and cultural issues which invite misery and destruction. Sometimes, technique without understanding leads to enmity and ruthlessness. So, it is commonly believed that advancement of science and technology leads to collapse of values. It is observed that misconceived notion of modernity and rapid growth of science and technology and subsequent industrialization have caused a great threat and danger to our old morals and values.

It is assumed that changes in our present society are unhealthy or they very often threaten the society by many problems. The traditional system and structures seem incapable to contend with present social problems. The supposition that we are in a period of social disintegration affects the conception of good (good man, good conduct, good education etc.). Values in conflict are also a common social happening. The alarming problems of society include problems like racism, war, sexism, poverty, pollution, exploitation, crime, corruption, population explosion, unemployment, illiteracy, inadequate health care, global warming, energy shortage etc. are somehow believed to be the result of social change and subsequent value degradation.

Variant social happenings affect economic growth, political strategy, environmental concern, religious distress etc. "Social changes is the transformation in the organization of society and in patterns of thoughts and behaviour over time" (Macionis, 1987:638).[7] Accordingly, we notice changes in values. In fact, social changes reshape values and in return emerging values also restructure social changes. Values are more fundamental than attitudes and opinions and exert greater influence on human and social behaviour. Values are the keys for better understanding of social changes. They play an important role in legitimating social, political and economic institutions and practices. Values are like variables for the enhanced approaching of social stability and change. "Society is a changing medium of creation and expression of his deep seated desires, values and aspirations."[8]

Social change incorporate cultural changes, changes due to conflict and tension, changes promoted by the need of adaptation and environmental factors, economic and political changes, demographic changes, technological and educational changes, religious and spiritual changes etc. On the other hand, values and beliefs have decisive impact on shaping social change. Ideas and values can cause change or be barriers to change, can be barriers at one time or promote change at another time. "All values, ideals and virtues are connected with man's sensitiveness to his ever-expansive, total environment…."[9] Interrelation among the elements of society and functions of these elements are guided by prevalent values. But these values have no meaning without any reference to society with all its ups and downs. Social changes often generate controversy and at that moment values are the only therapy to meet those matters.

Much has been written and spoken about the rapid rate of change that is characterizing our society. Nations around the world are experiencing dramatic shifts in their political, economic and social structures. Society is constantly in motion. It is viewed no longer a rigid structure or system; it is a soft meadow of relationships. We live in an era of striking social change. Moment after moment a man is confronted with new situations and problems. Even the sociological approaches to social change also have been changing.

A person has the capacity for reflective self-evaluation. In the true sense "Values are generated mainly from our purposes, aspirations, beliefs, attitudes, feelings, interests, convictions etc. having close link with society and environment around us."[10] There are some values which change according to the social change. New values may evolve from the fresh experiences of the individual in the form of concepts and principles. In examining, analyzing and understanding and more generally in evaluating society, we should connect social phenomena to these values. Values are important for social equilibrium. They have relative permanence and universality in comparison to change. In due course new set of values arises. "Our values do not change; but the ways and means of expressing them do."[11] Actually new settings and new contents of value arise.

All values adopted by men create exclusivity in human beings as these values are different for every society and indeed for every man. The values most often are the source of conflicts in the world as every person or nation believes strongly in their values as right. Some of them are non-permanent and transient which change with time and space. The values of the present generation are not exactly same as the values of the previous generation. Yet there is some ingredient in all values that never changes. It has remained same in long years of human evolution. These are called spiritual values (like love, compassion, justice, truth etc.). It is the nature of the man to imbibe these values irrespective of his religion, race, culture or nationality. These values are so universal that all human beings seem to understand it without being taught. The moral worth of a society is reflected in the values it cherishes, the ideals it pursues and its sincerity in upholding them.

"To whatever area, field or job we may belong to we cannot escape values."[12] Valuation plays an important role in man's social living. Beliefs and attitudes of a society are reflected on values. In a society values are ideals that guide or qualify one's (individual's) personal conduct and interaction with others. Values serve as straits of communication and rational discussion among members of a society. It is the value-system which has been attempting an integration and harmonization of the personal and social aspects of human life. Values reflect both the actual state of society and its aspirations. Values are always at the foundation of our policies and procedures of a particular situation. The "quality of life" or the "standard of life" is determined by the perpetual values of man and society. They must be regarded as interdependent processes in a complete configuration. For harmonious functioning of society, values are conceived with reference to needs and changes.

Notes

1. Mukerjee, R.K., 1950. *The Dynamics of Morals*. London: MacMillan & Co. Ltd., p. 86.
2. Bhattacharyya, H.M., 1959. *The Principles of Philosophy*. Calcutta: University of Calcutta, p. 385.
3. Haferkamp, H. and Smelser, N.J., 1993. In: Sztompka, P., *The Sociology of Social Change*. Wiley Blackwell, p. xiii.
4. Sztompka, P., 1993. *The Sociology of Social Change*. Wiley Blackwell, p. 4.
5. *Ibid.*, p. xiii.
6. Lenski and Lenski. 1993. In: Sztompka, P., *The Sociology of Social Change*. Wiley Blackwell. p. xiii.
7. Macionis, J.J., 1993. In: Sztompka, P., *The Sociology of Social Change*. Wiley Blackwell. p. 6.
8. Mukerjee, R.K., 1950. *The Dynamics of Morals*. London: MacMillan & Co. Ltd., p. xix.
9. *Ibid*, p. 209.
10. Gupta, N.L., 1992. *A Search for Human Values*. New Delhi: Arya Book Depot., p. iv.
11. Radhakrishnan, S., 1959. *Religion and Society*. London: George Allen & Unwin, p. 102
12. Gupta, N.L., 1992. *A Search for Human Values*. New Delhi: Arya Book Depot., p. iv.

5
Value Inculcation through Folk Tales

Folk tales exist in every culture. It is a category of traditional story that is orally passed down through generations. It is one area of folklore study and expressions. The folk tale is considered as an umbrella term. It accommodates many kinds of narrative forms that are produced and created by and for different communities and cultural groups primarily through the oral tradition. It is an apt medium to explain and understand the world.

Vivian Paley once said that storytelling is the most ancient of communal occupations. Generally, folk tales depict narratives of talking animals, royalty, peasants, or mythical creatures and feature morals or lessons. Often, the main characters of folk tales are animals instead of people. Folk tales also stimulate the imagination and reflect the unbroken communion of human life with the life universal. They usually have no identified author, but they mirror the values and culture of the society from which they originated.

Before 1450 when printing machine had not been invented story-telling was the suitable source of entertainment and education. Subsequently, folk tales in hard copy form helped to preserve the rich collection of folk tales floating around Europe. In the 1800s, Europeans began to record their cultural history by collecting regional folk tales into books. Joseph Jacobs from England, Wilhelm and Jacob Grimm from Germany, and Peter Asbjornsen and Moe Jorgen from Norway, were all early collectors of regional folk tales. Their collection of folk tales is still found in anthology and picture books throughout the world. Besides books, now-a-days various types of folk tales exist in the world in different forms through internet, newspaper, radio, television, cinematic version and other types of medium.

There is no concluding definition of value. But every living human being lives by certain values. The values present a true outlook of the development of any society or nation. They tell us to what extent a society or nation has developed itself. Values are virtues, ideals and qualities on which actions and beliefs are based. Values are guiding principles that shape our world outlook, attitudes and conduct. R. Mukerjee says, "Man's ends and values are modes of his adjustment to the rest of the universe that like his tools, language, traditions and other products are selected in the actual process of his living in societies" (Mukerjee, R., 1965:28). Values serve as criteria for selection in action, judgement, preference and choice. The constructive values like honesty, compassion, integrity, forgiveness, love, knowledge, discipline, faith, leadership etc. are encouraged in our societies.

The inculcation of human values is a process that aims to make a person perfect human being. Every child can be inculcated with human values by the parents, teachers, friends, well-wishers. During recent years inculcation of value in young has assumed increasing prominence in educational policies, programmes and discussions. Education in general and value education in particular occupies a prestigious place in the modern context of the contemporary society. Parents, teachers and society at large are concerned about values and value education of children. The main purpose of education, in this millennium, is to give special emphasis in man's dignity and values.

Inculcation of values is not a simple matter. There is no magic formula of it. Value education is planned educational action aimed at the development of proper attitudes, values, emotions and behaviour patterns of the learners. It covers all aspects of personality development—intellectual, social, moral, aesthetic and spiritual. Value education is not a subject or course; it is an integral part of the curriculum. NCERT makes a list of 84 values. Values are to be caught and not taught. Younger children and growing adolescent could catch values of elderly people. But now, a negative scenario is witnessed. So, values have got to be taught in addition to being caught.

Folk tales allow the reader or listener to gain insight into the values and customs of the society that had produced the particular oral tale. Popular folk tales reflect moral values in society and culture and also quicken the moral sentiments. These folk tales that passed down through succeeding generations have also reflected the changing moral values. In a folk tale, goodness is always rewarded. Heroes and heroines live happily ever after while villains are suitably punished. Throughout the generations, the story may change but its core remains the same.

According to Jane Yolen folk tales serve four basic functions in the education of every child—

(i) to provide a landscape for allusion;
(ii) a way to look at another culture from the inside out;
(iii) to be used for therapy; and
(iv) a framework or model for a individual's belief system.

Alice Abler points out that popular fairy tales have been used sometimes to educate and sometimes to frighten children (and adults) into compliance, graphically warning of the consequences for wrong actions. The stories often addressed fears of abandonment violence. Folk tales have social impact. They give children the freedom to use their imagination. Children can gain knowledge and experience to help them deal with various social situations that might come their way. A folk tale is used to explain natural phenomena or events of historic significance. Nina Jaffe, the author of *Tales of the Seventh Day* and many other folk tale books, says that folk tales give a way for people to see, feel and understand life from many different perspectives—both personal and cultural.

Bruno Bettelheim, the famous child psychologist feels that folk tales are irreplaceable as a use of enchantment for children. They serve to educate, support and liberate the emotions of children. They lead, direct and suggest the child to find his own solutions. Folk tales have the capacity to transform a diseased mind into a very fresh, innocent, healthy and attentive. Folk tales transform mind capable of higher sensitivity and a heightened level of perception. They help to think of oneself as an individual—good and useful member of society.

Cultural awareness and morality are two purposes of folk tales. Folk tales teach children about their heritage, culture and codes of behaviour. Folk tales inspire all the domains of learning—cognitive, affective and psychomotor. The folk tales have been an eternal part of every culture since ages. When it comes to Indian folk tales, the India, the country of diverse religions, languages and cultures has a complete range of folk tales. The interesting tales range from the remarkable '*Pañcatantra*' to '*Hitopadeśa*', from '*Jātaka*' to '*Akbar-Birbal*'. The great Indian epics like '*Rāmāyaṇa*' and '*Mahābhārata*' are full of didactic stories inspired from the lives of great souls. Being full of moralistic values, Indian folk tales make perfect stories for children to instil right values. All these ancient stories have been passed from generation to generation; creating bondage of traditional values with present-day generation. For example, the *Hitopadeśa*, composed by Nārāyaṇa Paṇḍit is a remarkable compilation of reader-friendly stories full of decent instructions to lead a good life. The *Jātaka* (Buddhist) tales also were meant for the mankind to gain knowledge and morality. Originally written in Pāli language, *Jātaka* tales have been translated in different languages around the world. The luminous fables of '*Jātaka*' are intended to impart values of self-sacrifice, morality, honesty and other informative values to people. In the same way, the purpose behind the composition the *Pañcatantra*, a legendary collection of stories written by Vishnu Sharma was to implant moral values and governing skills in the young sons of the king.

Values are to enjoy life, to help others to enjoy and these must be without harming anybody. Values are the guiding principles of life which are conducive to all-round development. They bring quality of life in terms of joy, satisfaction and peace of life. Children and young are ignorant and confused about values and existing value system. Socio-cultural and political changes give rise to value conflicts and dilemmas. A life without proper values will become chaotic. Value education instills in children a sense of humanism, a deep concern for the well-being of others. Values are either innate or acquired. Innate values are our inborn divine virtues such as love, peace, happiness, mercy and compassion and acquired values are like respect, humility, tolerance, responsibility, cooperation, honesty and simplicity and so on.

Despite man's progress and material prosperity, peace and happiness will elude him because of inward turmoil of feelings and attitudes. In more than 90 per cent of homes desirable value inculcation become impossible due to various reasons. A spirit of selfishness summons us everywhere. Television programmes and video games are taking the place of bedtime story rituals. There is almost a public debate on the erosion of values and education in functioning short of expectation in this regard. Even when books, newspapers, or computers are available, people use storytelling to share information and pass down their community's history, beliefs, and social expectations. Folk tales teach children lessons or values that are important to the success of a community or country. Storytelling and folk tales have always been and are very important in all world cultures. Throughout history, traditional cultures have recognized the role of storytelling in teaching values to children.

6

Indian Value System: Its Relevance in 21st Century

Max Müller has nobly confessed that if he were to look over the whole world to find out the country most richly endowed with all the wealth, power and beauty that nature can bestow-in some parts a very paradise on earth he should point to India. Yes, India was the heart of the East. In her influential tradition there was a close relationship between theory and practice, more precisely between theory and life. The main incentive of Indian philosophy is to experience and realize. It is a way of life. Therefore, Indian tradition is value centred, "Indian philosophy is essentially a philosophy of values" (Mahadevan, 1967: 152). The theoretical and the practical both functions of knowledge are clearly pointed out in Indian Philosophy. The theoretical reveals the existence of some object which is known as *Arthaparicchitti.* The practical helps in the attainment of some purpose in life and it is described as *phala-prāpti.* In India no sharp distinction can be made among philosophy, ethics and religion. The notion of value is the central thesis of these three. Therefore, Indian philosophy of value is unique. It is more perceptive and far deeper than the Western. It is not ready to separate theoretical thinking from the practical consequences.

Among three distinctive indicators: the doctrine of *Varṇas* (doctrine of four classes), the doctrine of *āśramas* (doctrine of four stages of life), and the doctrine of *puruṣārthas* (doctrine of four goals of life) the concept of *puruṣārtha* is an integrated approach to the value system. *Puruṣārtha* is the word in Indian philosophy for that which is value for the *Puruṣa* or finite individual (*puruṣaiḥ arthyate iti*). *Puruṣārtha* is "what is sought by man" (Hiriyanna, 1952:65). Variety of meanings gets associated with the *puruṣārtha* found in religio-philosophical texts. These range from motivations of human activities, human ends, individual urges, human needs, human pursuit etc.

The Indian tradition recognizes four ends and *puruṣārthas* to be pursued. They are *Kāma* or pleasure, *Artha* or wealth, *Dharma* or righteousness and *Mokṣa* or liberation. *Artha* and *Kāma* are secular or empirical values while *Dharma* and *Mokṣa* are spiritual. The concept of *puruṣārtha* has undoubtedly been quite conspicuous by its presence in almost the entire history of Indian thought. Various Indian thinkers have been agreed that there are certain ends or objects that are universally desired and sought. But sometimes they differ among themselves as to which of these is to be accorded the highest status in life. The word *puruṣārtha* is employed in dual sense; one may, "define a *puruṣārtha* as an end which is consciously sought to be accomplished either for its own sake or for the sake of utilizing it as a means to the accomplishment of a further end" (Hiriyanna, 1952:66). The goal of life is two-fold: *abhyudaya* (prosperity) and *niḥśreyasa* (highest bliss). *Abhyudaya* consists of *Dharma, Artha* and *Kāma.* These three are called *tri-varga*. They are to be pursued in the first two *āśramas*, *brahmacharya* and *gṛahastha.* The next two *āśramas*, *vānaprastha* and *saṁnyāsa* are to be devoted to the achievement of *niḥśreyasa* (*summum bonum*) and they consist in attaining *mokṣa* (salvation).

Kāma stands for psychological value. It is recognized as a psycho-biological force lying at the heart of creation. It is mentioned and accepted as a principle of enjoyment in various contexts in Indian literature. It inspires all human activities. For one's basic material well-being *kāma* is the steering force. *Kāmyate iti Kāma*—this lies in the root of any activity. "*Kāma* is a comprehensive term which stands for desires-desires ranging from the cravings of the flesh to the longing for the spirit" (Crawford, 1982:2). Natural desires and inclinations are the spring board of all human actions. Therefore, *kāma* is an important human value.

To fulfil or actualize our desire we need instrumentality of *Artha*. Most commonly, *Artha* signifies "that which can be perceived, an object of the senses". All objects of senses, desires, volitions, aspirations and actions are implied by the word *Artha*. *"Arthyate pratheyate iti artha"* literally means through which result is desired. In the value system instrumentality is closely attached with the meaning of *Artha*.

Sometimes desire for physical pleasure and aesthetic satisfaction (*kāma*) and wealth (*artha*) are looked down upon as low-grade value, because there is often a conflict between the sensual pleasure or acquisitions of wealth and duty. But the noticeable inferiority is actually ungrounded. Because all action is motivated by a desire and without some means of subsistence nobody can perform one's duties towards himself and society.

Dharma means "that which supports", right activity or duty, i.e. activity which is the result of a good-will. It is usually understood as the principle or law which sustains, supports or maintains (*dhārayati*) the individual as well as the social order. To obviate and adjudicate the conflict among desires *dharma* is needed as higher guiding principle. In its most frequent usages *dharma*, in the sphere of morality and ethics means "right way of living", "proper conduct", 'duty' or 'righteousness'. "The word *Dharma* has a much broader meaning and can be applied to cosmological regularity as well as human" (Basham, 2004:236).

The first three *puruṣārthas* (*dharma, artha* and *kāma*) are considered sufficient to lead a balanced social life for an individual. But the Indian seers did not stop here. They searched for the highest goal—*Mokṣa*. The Indian thinkers wanted to analyze and find out the origin, cause and means of annihilating suffering (*duḥkha*). All philosophical inquiry stared at the removal of this *duḥkha* and the very basis of *Mokṣa* lies in the concept of *duḥkha*. Different philosophical systems of India have defined *Mokṣa* differently. But, all the Indian philosophical systems (both theistic and non-theistic) are approximately unanimous about the suffering in life and its complete cessation. *Mokṣa* as *paramapuruṣārtha* tries to free life from all miseries.

In Indian philosophy, human life is inherently a spiritual process. Social and metaphysical aspects of human life are best framed in *puruṣārtha* scheme. "Ideally, every person should live a life filled with the joy and pleasure that attend the activities involved in satisfying one's needs and desires, which satisfaction presupposes a sufficiency of means for these activities. But, these activities are to be performed according to *dharma*, the moral rules governing man and the universe. By living such a life *Mokṣa* can be attained" (Crawford, 1982:23).

The Indian concept of *puruṣārtha* is a unique concept. It successfully performs the quite difficult task of classifying the total conceivable aspirations and objectives of the entire humanity into four distinct categories. In the scheme of *puruṣārtha* it is specifically proclaimed that in this set of four no one is either superfluous or exclusively cherishable. Accordingly, it puts an endeavour to secure a wonderful balance in an individual's life. The design of human pursuit in *puruṣārtha* tries to bring a notable synthesis between the real and the ideal, between secular and spiritual life; recognizing *Artha* and *Kāma* as ends of human life together with *Dharma* and *Mokṣa*. There is another implication that the eligibility for the pursuit of *Mokṣa* arises only after one has passed through the *trivarga* and realized the futility of worldly and other-worldly pleasures. The Indian philosophy of value proclaims two ways to attain integrated development of personality—the path of activity (*pravṛtti mārga*) and the path of renunciation (*nivṛtti mārga*). The main objective of *nivṛtti mārga* is seeking individual's spiritual perfection. The aspirant of this path requires giving up all his egotistic activities. According to *pravṛtti mārga,* it is quite possible to attain perfection for an individual by discharging all his duties, both social and individual. These duties necessarily include all duties arising from one's station (*varṇa*) and stage (*āśrama*) as laid down by scriptures. *Pravṛtti mārga* indicates an action oriented philosophy of life as it asserts a world affirmative attitude. In due course Indian thought and scriptures (particularly, *Upaniṣads* and *Gītā*) synthesize the two paths.

Puruṣārthas are organically related to human nature. We cannot deny that every human being tends for some type of liberation (*mokṣa*) and follows some natural laws (*dharma*), uses certain economic means (*artha*), and has certain instincts (*kāma*). Till man lives, *Puruṣārthas* are going to add meaning. They are positive and life affirming significant elements in Indian philosophical legacy. Indian value system is the combination of different natural, moral and spiritual values which provides norms to our behaviour. Indian value system brings about a synthesis of the social and economic, the emotional and spiritual life. All four values are set in an integrated fashion that each has its specific role and place in the ordering of human personality. Rounded personality and efficient society both are attempted throughout the scheme. To view man-in-society completely *puruṣārtha* pattern is exceptional contribution of Indian tradition. The four *puruṣārthas* need to be held together in a balanced interdependent way to maintain harmony in both individual and social life.

The social philosophy of India has been an attempt to help in blending the metaphysical and social aspects of human personality. After a sincere study of the *puruṣārtha* scheme, it is quite clear that there is an undercurrent of ancient universal values with the changes and adoption through ages in our social order. Present scenario is that we understand almost everything except who we fundamentally are. So, theory of *puruṣārtha* is relevant to today's man who wants to live a good life. Though *puruṣārtha* is set long ago by Indian sages and seers, yet it has been playing its distinctive role in moulding the spiritual development of individual personality and social growth.

The ancient Indian theory of *Kāma* is still relevant for our modern lifestyle. Sexuality is closely related to the formation of love bonds and to procreation. Sex is a responsibility. It is a positive pursuit. Society is nothing but an enlarged family. "A nation is made up of families bound together by steady marriage and happy homes. The sanctity of the marriage and homes determines the greatness of a nation" (Devadoss, 1979: 82). Today's sex life becomes cheap and trifling. But, sex should be experienced. Then only one can touch the spirit. Still marriage and sex life are not ready to abandon religious customs. As *Kāma* embodies sexual and non-sexual pleasure, literature such as poetry, drama, novel etc., music, art form, dance all these mesmerize us, touch our heart, take us to a different world and inspire us to keep aside our worldly agonies. At the present time film, dance theatres all these entertaining means are experimented and revolutionized in such a way that they are able to keep aside our worldly agonies. Modern man as he is busy in the competitive world definitely will get a rare kind of satisfaction to relieve his stress and anxiety if he spends few hours a week amidst such creative work. Today's fashion world can be linked with man's pleasure seeking pursuit. *Kāma* can be either a means to liberation and happiness in life or a great cause of suffering depending upon how we approach the same.

By recognizing *artha* as a value, the Indian traditional value perspective wants to draw attention to the view that every person has a right to earn his livelihood, to accumulate wealth and property. Material prosperity helps in the advancement of knowledge. Wealth played a great part in the building-up of civilization. In a prosperous country where people are content, there only the science, art and knowledge will flourish. Wealth is not only for one's own sake. *Dāna* or almsgiving is an imperative virtue of Indian tradition. But, it is warned that *Mahābhārata* says, "*Dāna* of wealth acquired unjustly (*anyāya śamupāttena*) does not free the donors from future dangers" (*Mbh.*, 3.245.32).

Kauṭilya had mentioned that wealth should be taken as *a good* not as *the good.* Indian conception of value not only regards wealth and property as essential element to lead human life, but indispensable building block of good life. Fame, praise, honour, recognition, happiness all follow wealth. "Money is sought as a means to all kinds of ends, high as well as low, spiritual as well as material" (Marshall, 1992:18). Wealth is a means to achieve something; it is a means for acquiring many objects for fulfilling desires. Individual's life has to be economically secured, and then only one can think about the higher spiritual life. For progress in life all the economical values and psychological values play a vital role. *Kāma* and *Artha* have acquired the place in the Indian value system because of social aspect attached to it. If *Kāma* is not treated as a *puruṣārtha,* society will lose all its moorings and humanity will become a butt of all the jokes. Apparently though traditional value '*Artha*' does not conform to modern economic theory, still both aim at the same. The goal is social progress and perfection. Though profit making is the target of business, curriculum of business management study is including Indian values to deal human nature and relation.

Modern economic environment aims at material first than spiritual. Due to this situation all unrest occupied our life and society miserably. So, *Artha* should be guided by *Dharma*. Property should be earned by rightful way then only it can justify itself as value. If it is used for self-indulgence, it will not be for spiritual progress. Again, if it is concentrated in the hands of few, corruption, poverty and discrimination will swallow the whole human race. In modern state, criminal laws are there to forbid increasing of property by anti-social activities. There are other preventive measures to spot illegal possessions and wealth. One's wealth and wealth acquiring method should not obstruct the progress of his fellow men—this is relevant irrespective of time and space. Today, we live in an age of free markets and a world economy. More people and nations are working together to spread freedom and democratic principles; to nurture free markets and to protect individual property right. Though the profit motive of business is understood and accepted, people should not accept it as an excuse for ignoring the basic norms, values and standards of being a good citizen.

Dharma was explicitly defined in terms of certain duties and obligations which were codified in the great law books to maintain the social order. Individual, society and nation can prosper following the path of *dharma* (in the sense of moral virtue, duties and code of conduct). In all stages of human life either as a student or as a householder, as a forest dweller or an ascetic, *Dharma* has to be accepted as paramount. We observe *Dharma* in the sense of duty even today. Social stability, justice, welfare, harmony, integration, well-being etc. are just other names for *Dharma*. Though *Varṇa dharma* cannot keep correspondence with the secular form of society, but it sheds light on a new direction towards social responsibility and stability. If we consider *Varṇa* as class, no class is less essential. On the basis of this system, the faculties, the talents, aptitudes and skills were perpetually promoted. But, in due course of time, the real purpose of the class system was hampered mainly due to economic exploitation of one class on other.

At present, corruptions, material prosperity by dishonest means, lying, stealing, exploitation, crimes of all kind are increasing rapidly. People are divided in the name of caste, community and religion and it is causing serious threat to national integration. All these are result of abandoning the right path, i.e. the path of *dharma*. Ruler ought to rule his country following the principle of righteousness. Kauṭilya's *Arthaśāstra* declares that ideal king regards the happiness of his subjects as his own happiness which can be realized only through the practice of *dharma*. In modern time justice, equality, human rights etc. are new terms and looks on the face of righteousness. Instead of ancient king new term 'government' comes to the scene. All the duties and responsibilities of ancient king are in this or that form existing in terms of acts and policies of government. Leaders of political parties, executive head of the state, administrative and judicial officers are bound to do their duties or follow right ways to discharge their responsibilities for smooth progress of the country. This situation cannot be termed as ancient or modern.

To live a good life is everyone's concern. Science and technology also aims at the enhancement of quality of life. But, 'Good earth' cannot be defined in terms of material possessions. The achievements of science with perceptible effects have changed our living style. But, in this modern technological world something is felt missing and that missing something can be named 'peace of mind'. The virtues categorized as *Sādhāraṇa dharma* are still relevant to the modern society. They are virtues like *Dhṛti* or fortitude, *Kṣamā* or forbearance, *Dama* or control over mind, *Asteya* or earning money by rightful means or strict adherence to one's own possessions without desire to take another's, *Śauca* or purity in thought, word and deed, *Indriyanigraha* or control over sense organs, *Dhī* or clarified understanding or intellect, *Vidyā* or knowledge of truth or education, *Satya* or truthfulness, *Akrodha* or freedom from anger etc. and these should be practiced by all, irrespective of their age, sex, social status etc. Social values like charity, honesty, truthfulness, sympathy for animal etc. are contributions of Indian value philosophy.

Recently, higher is the quantity of consumption, better is the quality of life. The value crisis in society is mainly due to excessive overplaying of the importance of material value of life and consequent downplaying of moral and spiritual values. People become right conscious, not duty conscious. Corruption, conflict and stress of present day society in the field of business, agricultural policies, politics, economics, education and other human activities can be played down by following the virtues of righteousness. In yester century Gandhi boldly declared that politics without morality is an offense.

Philosophy arose in India as a result of an enquiry into the mystery of life and existence. The life-centre of Indian culture is its spirituality. *Mokṣa* is the waking-up of human consciousness at the highest level of reality. It is total destruction of egoism. In the *jīvanmukti* or the embodied release, the liberated works for the good of the humanity without moral obligation. *Jīvanmukta* looks for the goal of universal welfare without attachment to finite fruit. In other words, the concept of value in every sphere grows out of the idea of self-realization. Traditional *Mokṣa* is identified in modern days with social, political and economic freedom and more precisely with peace. Modern society and individual are quite familiar with physical freedom. For them, freedom means political, economical, social, constitutional etc. They are totally ignorant of spiritual freedom. Political, economical, social, constitutional freedoms are fragmentary aspects of real freedom. Spiritual freedom is freedom from hatred, greed, ignorance, violence, fear and so on. Individuals are putting importance only on physical freedom. But, these are only means, not the ultimate freedom. Ultimate end is spiritual freedom. Pure happiness comes only through this freedom and it will lead to eternal peace. Our self—more exactly our spirit never put off the divine dress. So, we in 21st century speak of business ethics, medical ethics, environmental ethics, geo-ethics, human rights, sustainable development, ecological consciousness and invite traditional values to regulate all these.

All values adopted by men create exclusivity in human beings as these values are different for every society and indeed for every man. The values are thus the source of conflicts in the world as every person or nation believes strongly in their values as right. Such values are non-permanent and transient which changes with time and space. The values of the present generation are not same as the value of the previous generation. Yet there is some ingredient in all values that never changes. It has remained same in long years of human evolution. These values are eternal as they never change. Therefore, often people call such values as spiritual or divine as it never dies; like love, compassion, justice, truth etc. It is the nature of the man to imbibe these values irrespective of his religion, race, culture or nationality. These values are so universal that all human beings seem to understand it without being taught. To build a future without tradition is anti-historical; we usually pursue those values which have been handed down to us by our culture.

The modern world has been moving more and more towards individualistic values where the interest of the individual is considered to be the most 'right' and needs to be protected over everything else. But, "If we can discover some means of giving full expression to deep human instincts and interests, and sublimate and redirect those which are harmful; if we can discover a social order based on human needs and human nature and not merely on commercial, industrial and economic motives, a social order in which there shall be higher values than work and wages, comforts and luxuries.......then progress rather than decay may lie ahead of us in this century" (Patrick, 1910:25). The truthful interplay of traditional and modern values or proper assimilation of these noble ideals and values by preserving, reformulating and extending will definitely make India wealthier both materially and spiritually.

Section II

Social Issues and Valuation

7
Eco-Feminism: A Brief Outline

More simply eco-feminism is an analysis and a social movement. It is a relatively new part of the feminist movement. The term 'eco-feminism' is the conjunction of the words 'ecology' and 'feminism', a critique that draws parallels between the suppression of women and nature. Eco-feminists attack dualistic thinking of patriarchal society. Some of common dualisms addressed by eco-feminists are male/female, culture/nature and mind/body. Eco-feminism seeks to move beyond this dualistic worldview and restructure the notion of power. The movement wants to create an interconnected community, void of hierarchies, where all beings—human, non-human, and members of the organic world have their own intrinsic value. They all are considered as parts of the same living organism, the Earth.

"Ecological feminism is essentially a response to a set of key problems thrown-up by the two great social currents of the later part of (the last) century-feminism and the environmental movement" (Plumwood, 1993:10). Eco-feminism is an important current in philosophical, theological opinion and social analysis. It perceives an interconnection between the domination of women and the domination of nature. The single shared premise to which all eco-feminists would ascribe is the idea that there is a link between the oppression of women and the oppression of nature. This interconnection occurs on two levels: the ideological-cultural level and the socio-economic level. On the ideological-cultural level, it is said that women are 'closer to nature' than the male, who are more associated with the body, matter and the emotions. On the socio-economic level, women are located in the sphere of reproduction, with child-raising, with the preparation of food, with washing clothes and housework, roles that are devalued in relation to the public sphere of power and culture of males. The social movement of eco-feminism which arises out of this analysis seeks to end this interconnected oppression, and argues that one cannot have an effective environmentalism which is not feminist, or an effective feminism which is not environmentalist.

In fact, there is no one-accepted or orthodox eco-feminism. Eco-feminism, sometimes named as a "new term for an ancient wisdom" that grew out of various social movements—the feminist, peace and ecology movements in the late 1970s and early 1980s. It emerged as numerous forms of feminist and environmental theories and activism intersected. As Karen Warren notes eco-feminism is an umbrella term for a wide variety of approaches. The term was introduced by Francoise d'Eaubonne in her book *Le Feminisme on la Mort* (Feminism or Death) published in 1974. In her article titled *The Time for Eco-Feminism*, Francoise d'Eaubonne explained that this new global movement within feminism draws upon the specifically feminine power to combat the ecological crisis and the systems of male dominance that have given rise to it. The *Women and Life on Earth: Eco-feminism in the Eighties*, conference held at Amherst (1980) was the first of a series of eco-feminist conferences inspiring the growth of eco-feminist organization and actions.

Eco-feminism is never a reality, vision or practice. It is a convergence of the ecological and feminist analyses and movements. It wraps many items in its package. Yenestra King, prominent eco-feminist, named it a third wave of feminism. Others describe and put it in the general category of deep ecology. Eco-feminism simultaneously serves as an environmental critique of feminism and a feminist critique of environmentalism. Eco-feminist books became popular and created larger definitions of what eco-feminism means. In the course of time, people in philosophy, sociology, political science, religion, ethics, economics and environmental and women studies shaped the eco-feminist discourse. Rosemary Radford Reuther, Ivone Gebara, Vandana Shiva, Susan Griffine, Alice Walker, Starhawk, Sallie Mcfague, Luisah Teish, Sun Ai Lee Prak, Paula Gunn Allen, Monica Sjoo, Greata Gaard, Karen Warren and Andy Smith are among the voices speaking for eco-feminist positions.

Eco-feminism is an activist and academic movement that see critical connections between the domination of nature and the exploitation of women. It asserts that all forms of oppression are connected and that structures of oppression must be addressed in their totality. "Women must see that there can be no liberation for them and no solution to the ecological crisis within a society whose fundamental model of relationships continues to be one of domination. They must unite the demands of the women's movements with those of the ecological movement to envision a radical reshaping of the basic socio-economic relations and underlying values of this (modern industrial) society" (Ruether, 1975: 204).

Eco-feminism claims that patriarchal structures justify their dominance through categorical or dualistic hierarchies: heaven/earth, mind/body, male/female, human/animal, spirit/matter, culture/nature, white/non-white. All dualisms and binary oppositional forms must be dismantled otherwise humanity remains divided against it. Three connections seem central to eco-feminist: the empirical, the conceptual and or cultural or symbolic and the epistemological. The empirical claim is that in most part of the world environmental problems generally disproportionately affect women. Women and nature are connected conceptually and or culturally or symbolically. Dualistic structure implies that men have innate power over both women and nature. This dualistic structure identifies women with feminity, the body, Earth, sexuality and flesh and men with masculinity, spirit, mind and power. The eco-feminist epistemological claim follows from the connection between women and nature. Women have more knowledge about earth systems than men. So, women are in a privileged position to aid in creating new practical and intellectual ecological paradigms.

Eco-feminism advocates turning toward nature reclaiming the connection to protect the interest of the natural world and to empower women physically, spiritually and economically. During the three decades (1970-2000) eco-feminist activists engaged in numerous protests, boycotts and campaigns to bring attention to the inter-connection of justice issues related to women and environment as a whole. Eco-feminism became popular only in the context of numerous protests and activities against environmental destruction.

Karen Warren in her *Eco-Feminist Philosophy* puts that eco-feminism is all connected. Yes, imperialism, ecological degradation, exploitation of workers, racism and women's oppression, etc. all these are interwoven. In her *Feminism and Ecology: Making Connections*, Warren has argued for a basic eco-feminist position: that feminism ought to pay attention to environmental issues and ecological interdependencies and that environmentalists ought to attend to the connections among ecological degradation, sexism and other forms of social oppression. Warren used the tools of analytical philosophy to articulate and argue for eco-feminism as a philosophical position, ethical approach and political movement.

The concept was, appearing throughout 1970s with authors like Rosemary Ruether's *New Women New Earth—Sexist Ideologies and Human Liberation* (1975), Susan Griffin's *Women and Nature—The Roaring Inside Her* (1978) and Carolyn Marchant's *The Death of Nature—Women Ecology and Scientific Revolution* (1980) and Mary Daly's *Gny/Ecology* (1979). Their adaptation of feminism was heavily rooted in the environmental or green movement and peace movements of the 1970s. A series of documents and publications in the 1980s by NGOs, donor agencies and scholars writing in relatively popular presses forwarded a strong view that women were the primary users and managers of the environment at the local level. It was argued that women's work, especially in reproductive and subsistence-focused activities involves them closely with the environment and its resources, as hewers of wood, haulers of water and cultivators of food. Women were seen to have responsibilities which make them closely dependent on and give them distinct interests in natural resources, especially as sources of food and fuel. This in turn was deemed to give women deep and extensive environmental knowledge and experiential expertise. In the early 1980s, there was much emphasis on women as victims of environmental degradation. Women were conceptualized as the central agents of primary environmental care, which linked caring for the environment, meeting basic needs and community empowerment.

Since the late 1970s and 1980s, eco-feminism has split into a number of subdivisions based on different theoretical perspectives on women's relationship to nature and the root causes of the oppression of each. As put by Carolyn Marchant different types of eco-feminism are:

(i) Liberal eco-feminism which takes an equality of opportunity approach to social and environmental change.
(ii) Socialist eco-feminism which blends Marxist theoretical analyses with analyses of the links between women and nature.
(iii) Social eco-feminism which follows from American anarchist Murray Bookchin's philosophy of social ecology.
(iv) Cultural eco-feminism which avoids masculine modifiers and is based instead on women's innate connections to the earth and natural processes of life.
(v) Spiritual eco-feminism which looks at goddess religions and women's spiritual relationship to the environment.
(vi) Post-modern eco-feminism is the branch which questions not only the validity of the concept of the environment but of women as well.

Warren says that eco-feminism is based on the following general claims: "(1) There are important connections between the oppression of women and the oppression of nature. (2) Understanding the nature of these connections is necessary to any adequate understanding of the oppression of women and the oppression of nature. (3) Feminist theory and practice must include an ecological perspective. (4) Solutions to ecological problems must include a feminist perspective" (Warren, 1987:4-5).

Throughout our history nature is portrayed as feminine and women are often thought of as closer to nature than men. Women's physiological connection with birth and child care has partly led to this close association with nature. Eco-feminism is the belief that the social mentality that leads to the domination and oppression of women is directly connected to the social mentality that leads to the abuse of the environment. It is based on the notion that women are especially "close to nature" in a spiritual or conceptual sense. "[Women] conceived of their own bodies as being productive and creative in the same way as they conceived of external nature as being productive and creative... They co-operate with their bodies and with the earth in order to 'let grow and make grow' " (Mies, 1986: 56).

Various responses to the women nature link exist. Women and nature are connected in morally significant ways. Both are identified with feminity. Women and nature are connected as providers of life, sustenance and creativity, they are similarly important and valuable and their strengths are similarly controlled or violated by men (or patriarchy). But some claim that the link should be deconstructed and contested. Others claim that it should be celebrated and honoured and some other considers it to be the part of past rather than present history. Eco-feminism has not been without critics—from eco-feminist themselves as well as from others. Eco-feminism has also been criticized for failing to embrace diversity among women. Its criticism results from its lack of clarity as a theory. Some of the most ardent critics question the women/nature link that is sometimes placed at the core of eco-feminism. Sherry Ortner's essay—*Is Female to Male as Nature is to Culture* (1974) is such evidence. Some feminist critics of eco-feminism took the fact that woman in a constructed category to indicate that women nature connections are ultimately only cultural and symbolic. Others also argue that the very idea of women nature connections suggests a limiting conception of feminity and a false sense of female superiority. Various feminists distance themselves from eco-feminism because of strong women nature connection assumed and developed in some eco-feminist positions. Such feminists suggest that it is an essentialist position. Many eco-feminists count themselves as deep ecologists while others might designate themselves as one but not the other. An area of eco-feminism that needs to be addressed is the connection with animal rights activism. Greta Gaard's anthology "*Eco-Feminism: Women, Animals, Nature*" includes several essays that analyze the mutual oppressions of women and non-human animals in patriarchal societies.

Eco-feminist arguments have served to inspire a large range of social and environmental movements, ranging from specific forms of grassroots activism around the environment. It contains both a critique of the dominant "patriarchal conceptual framework" and offers a feminist framework that is "grounded in familiar ecological principles". According to many eco-feminists, patriarchalism leads to the destruction of the Earth. Eco-feminists maintain that since we are human beings, we can only understand how to behave towards non-human beings in terms of principles and insights that are derived from the particular character of our humanity.

Noted eco-feminist from India Vandana Shiva plays a major role in the global eco-feminist movement. According to her article *Empowering Women,* Shiva suggests that a more sustainable and productive approach to agriculture can be achieved through reinstating a system of farming in India that is more centred on engaging women. She advocates against the prevalent "patriarchal logic of exclusion" claiming that a woman-focused system would change the current system in an extremely positive manner.

Women must see that there can be no liberation for them and no solution to the ecological crisis within a society whose fundamental model of relationships continues to be one of domination. They must unite the demands of the women's movement with those of the ecological movement to envision a radical reshaping of the basic socio-economic relations and the underlying values of this [modern industrial] society (Ruether, 1975: 204).

Bina Agarwal describes four main overlying percepts in eco-feminism: the first is the exploration of the commonalities between gender oppression and environmental degradation. The second states that men are more related to culture and that women are related to environment. Thirdly, oppression of women and the oppression of nature have occurred simultaneously and thus women have a responsibility to cease male domination over both. Fourthly, eco-feminism seeks to combine feminism and ecological thought as they both work towards egalitarian, non-hierarchical structures.

In academic circles eco-feminism began to be understood in four ways: as the history of women-nature association, as a lens through which many disciplines (sociology, psychology, technology etc.) could be refocused, as an alliance within ecological, political and social movements and as a way how women concerns (poverty, childcare, ethnicity, sexual assault, health etc.) are related to the beliefs about what is natural or to environmental degradation. Within industrially developed societies, eco-feminists debate the issue of gender difference within cultures in conversation with movements such as deep ecology, anti-militarism, animal liberation, anti-racism, and environmental justice. Eco-feminists consistently review the environmental effects of gendered science and resource management, together with economic development models that have a disproportionate and often disastrous impact on women. "Eco-feminism is about connectedness and wholeness of theory and practice. It asserts the special strength and integrity of every living thing........" (King, 1983:10). Nevertheless eco-feminism offers a potentially transformative philosophy of the self and of society. It is now interdisciplinary, multifocal, all encompassing and comprehensive that almost everybody and every concern are included.

8
Conflict, Conflict Resolution and National Integration

Basically conflict means disagreement. A conflict is an opposition of people, forces, or other entities. It is actual or perceived opposition of needs, values and interests. A conflict can be even internal (within oneself) to individuals. In several cases, conflict seems to be a fact of life. "Conflict is a theme that has occupied the thinking of man more than any other, save only God and Love" (Rapoport, 1960:12). It is an antagonistic state or action which usually contains substantive, procedural and psychological dimensions. We all have seen situations where different people with different goals and needs have come into conflict. A conflict is more than mere disagreement—it is a situation in which people perceive a threat (physical, emotional, power, status, etc.) to their well-being. Conflicts occur when people (or other parties) perceive that, as a consequence of a disagreement, there is a threat to their needs, interests or concerns. Although conflict is a normal part of organizational life, providing numerous opportunities for growth through improved understanding and insight, there is a tendency to view conflict as a negative experience caused by abnormally difficult circumstances.

Conflict can exist at a variety of levels:

- intrapersonal conflict,
- interpersonal conflict,
- group conflict,
- organizational conflict,
- community conflict,
- intra-state conflict,
- international conflict and so on.

Conflict resolution is a process of working through opposing views in order to reach a common goal or mutual purpose. It is about how to deal with conflicts among people. Conflict resolution is a range of methods of eliminating sources of conflict. The term 'conflict resolution' is sometimes used interchangeably with the term dispute resolution or alternative dispute resolution. Processes of conflict resolution generally include negotiation, mediation, and diplomacy. The processes of arbitration, litigation, and formal complaint processes are usually described with the term dispute resolution, although some refer to them as conflict resolution. Processes of mediation and arbitration are often referred to as alternative dispute resolution.

Historically, conflict resolution has evolved in 1950s and 1960s as a result of the development of nuclear weapons. The conflicts between superpowers at the height of Cold War very often used to threaten human survival. So, different scholars from different disciplines move towards the study of conflict as a general phenomenon. Conflict resolution relates to all domains of conflicts, whether within or between families, organizations, communities or countries. It is a broad and fast growing academic field. "Conflict Resolution is about ideas, theories and methods that can improve our understanding of conflict and our collective practice of reduction in violence and enhancement of political processes for harmonizing interest" (Bercovitch, *et al.*, 2009:1).

We are not going to give either any particular list of prevalent conflicts or detailed exposition of the theories of conflict resolution. Accepting conflict as a fact here we try to understand the idealistic milieu of conflict resolution and its relation to national integration. The philosophy behind it is that we should not let the conflict to control us. If conflict is not handled effectively, the results can be hurtful. Conflicting goals will quickly turn into personal dislike. Teamwork breaks down. Talent is wasted as people extricate from their work. Then it becomes easy to end up in a vicious descending. Preventing and resolving conflict before it results in violence is far less costly, both in human and financial terms. Action to address the underlying causes of conflict include strengthening governance, improving access to human rights, economic and social development, destruction of weapons and developing a culture of peace.

"Any conflict is like a cancer. The sooner it is resolved the better for all the parties concerned in particular and society in general. If it is not resolved at the earliest possible opportunity, it grow at a very fast pace, and with time it effort required to resolve it increases exponentially as new issues emerge and conflicting situation proliferate. One dispute leads to another. It is essential to resolve the dispute the moment it rears its head" (Agrawal, 2005:3). Four key components of conflict resolution are: Controlling emotional responses, Seeking understanding, Identifying needs and common interests and Seeking mutual benefit or purpose.

S. Radhakrishnan says that National Integration is not a house which could be built by mortar and bricks. It is not an industrial plan too which could be discussed and implemented by experts. Integration, on the contrary is a thought which must go into the hearts of all the people. It is the consciousness which must awaken the people at large. National Integration is a positive aspect. It is primarily a political concern. It reduces socio-cultural and economic differences or inequalities and strengthens national unity and solidarity, which is not imposed by any authority. The thought of National integrity and Unity is not something that can be achieved by enacting a law or proposing a theory or presenting a paper or discussion in a seminar or in a newspaper publication.

India got independence on 15th August, 1947, but it was "broken *swaraj*" parting India and Pakistan. Immediately after partition both the nations had witnessed three bloody wars (in 1948, 1965, and 1971). The newly independent India was itself at calamitous strait of consolidating its own post-independent position during the decades to follow – trauma of blood bath during the partition, continuous war with two neighbouring countries, and creation of Bangladesh. Till that time India has been craving for national integration. But the cyclone of violence has today taken its own course affecting not only the normative fabric of social lives, but has also jeopardized the democratic practices in the region.

Territorially, we have been integrated. India is politically integrated through the various constitutional bodies. It is also judicially integrated from the village court to the Supreme Court. Educational Councils also brought out educational integration. Administrative integration is also achieved through the system of Civil Services. Still the question of national integration remains unsolved as the psychological integration is lacking. "Sadly what is lacking in the whole process of psychological integration is the imperative of mutual recognition and respect for the value system of communities other than one's" (Malla, 1998:21).

Communalism, lingual conflict and regionalism are the main challenges to national integration. Even if we put a casual eye on the socio-political scenario of North-East region, our own land we witness frequent inter-ethnic or inter-community rivalry, hatred and bloodshed. Naga insurgence, which started in the 1950s, known as the mother of the North-east insurgencies, is one of the oldest unresolved armed conflicts in the world. In total, Manipur, Assam, Nagaland and Tripura have witnessed scales of conflict. Currently, most of the states in the region are also affected by some form of domestic conflicts. It can be said that the north-east people are in conflict between and among themselves.

At another level, conflict in the region has been an all-pervasive phenomena, and in its violent form, it has not only affected the territorial and political sovereignty of the Indian state, but also the life of the various people living in the region in incomprehensible and inexplicable terms. Let us say in the words of Clemens Spiess, that the various problems and conflict constellations in the North-east "represent(s) durable challenges to the integrative and accommodative capacity of Indian democracy". Since independence, the Indian State and society has constantly been challenged by forces of fundamentalism, violence, conflict and terror. Even today ethnic and communal crises were not extinct. Currently, these conflicts have got very popular and new terms such as 'Identity assertion', 'Ethno-nationalism movement', 'Freedom movement', 'Self-determination movement', 'Homeland demand' and like that. The rising ethnocentrism becomes the biggest challenge ever faced by the human society today. We may say that the conflicts and tensions we experience now can be considered as the outcome of ethnocentrism.

Again, the growing insurgency is a major problem for the Indian Government (For example, in 2003, the Maoists had influence over 55 districts in 9 states; it is now estimated that they have established their writ over 223 districts in 20 states in India) and these conflicts posit internal security challenges waging war against national integration.

Indian Constitution has defined and declared the common goal for its citizens as "to secure to all the citizens of India Justice—social, economic and political—liberty equality and fraternity". The notion of national integration denotes that all citizens irrespective of caste, creed and colour are equal and are free to adopt any economic profession and mode of worship and should respect the mutual rights and independence of their fellow country man. India has been trying to resolve conflicts through her secular ideology. Diplomacy is an effective tool of conflict resolution. But it should rest on a norm of co-existence allowing to live and let live. Co-existence means equal rights. The norms of co-existence smooth the progress of conflict resolution. Conflict Resolution is commitment to peace. Peace building is a term used to describe the processes and activities involved in resolving violent conflict and establishing a sustainable peace. It is an overarching concept that includes conflict transformation, restorative justice, trauma healing, reconciliation, development, and leadership, underlain by spirituality. Peace building includes promoting conflict resolution and reconciliation techniques. Chic Dambach, President & CEO, Alliance for Peace building once said that the ultimate objective of peace building is to reduce and eliminate the frequency and severity of violent conflict.

Negotiation would ensure a platform where voluntary and non-pressured dialogue could be initiated. It is extremely important to have an open dialogue where contending parties are relatively at ease. The idea of reconciliation as moral initiative can be successfully initiated only when the moral agents who are party to the negotiations are free from constraints. Conciliation and reconciliation are moral concepts and can be meaningfully engaged only through morally free actions. The idea is to suggest for morally driven political choices and actions. Now-a-days, alternative dispute resolution has become a global necessity. In recent times, this type of resolution has emerged as a significant movement in conflict management. The main methods of alternative dispute resolution are negotiation, mediation, conciliation and arbitration.

The truth is that by resolving conflict successfully, one can solve many of the problems that it has come to the surface, as well as getting benefits that might not been expected at first. In the long run this will encourage integrity. The significant effects of conflict resolution are like:

(i) **Increased understanding:** The discussion needed to resolve conflict expands people's awareness of the situation, giving them an insight into how they can achieve their own goals without undermining those of other people.

(ii) **Increased group cohesion:** When conflict is resolved effectively, team members can develop stronger mutual respect and a renewed faith in their ability to work together.

(iii) **Improved self-knowledge:** Conflict pushes individuals to examine their goals in close detail, helping them understand the things that are most important to them, sharpening their focus, and enhancing their effectiveness.

Conflict is normal, ever-present, unavoidable and useful on occasion. The fact that conflict exists, is not necessarily a bad thing. It is an inherent feature of human existence. It is difficult to conceive of a situation which is conflict free. But conflict refers either to a violent dispute or to an incompatibility of positions. Therefore, it should be resolved. If it is resolved effectively, it can lead to personal and professional growth. This notion cannot be eliminated from the heart of human societies. The only thing that can be eliminated is the violent expression of conflict. The new field of conflict resolution is one of the most interdisciplinary of all academic fields. It is a vibrant field of enquiry.

The concerned national and state authorities should readily attend the feeling of neglect and deprivation, the substantial regional imbalance, economic inequalities, to strengthen the spirit of integration. Effective conflict resolution is a process of cementing tie to feel oneness as equal members of one great family. Today's nationalism of India revolves around the moulding of diverse nationalities, language and culture groups into one great country. Even after 70 years of independence we are still looking forward for the processes of national integration to be completed. We, everyone should learn to appreciate beauty of diversity in unity.

9

Education and Dimension of Human Personality

Education is considered as a lifelong process of development by which an individual gradually adopts himself in various ways to the physical, social and spiritual environment. J. Krishnamurti in *Education and the Significance of Life* says that revolt is of two kinds: there is violent revolt, which is mere reaction, without understanding against the existing order; but there is an intelligent revolt, which is not reaction and which comes with self-knowledge through the awareness of one's own thought and feeling. We may put education in the second kind of revolt.

Since Vedic age, the aim of proper education had been the all round development of humanity. Education is a new outlook of life; it is a second birth. It is a search for wholeness. In the *Gurukul* system of education, a student spent a simple and well regulated life. For the full development of inner and outer talent of the *śiṣya,* it was accepted essential to bring the education in early age. In that system, complete knowledge of a particular subject was aimed at after the general knowledge of various needful subjects. At the same time, more references were there regarding character building and social prosperity. We all know that in Vedic literature education was described that which leads one from unreal to real, from darkness to light, from death to immortality. Particularly, the *Upaniṣadic* writings constitute the first regularly recorded instances of the adventures of human mind with curiosity and imagination to find answer to the fundamental aspects such as Creation, Ultimate Reality, human existence and self-realization.

At present, our education system makes us proficient in some branch of knowledge. But, it seems to emphasize only secondary values. This may lead to confusion and ruthlessness. Now, we are caught in the machine of competition to develop efficiency. Acquiring knowledge, gathering and correlating facts are everything in present-day education. The education system overemphasizes technique. The exclusive cultivation of technique produces scientists, mathematicians, space conquerors and like, but it is doubtful how these specialists experience life as a whole. It seems that present education makes one subservient and mechanical. Gradually, the individual begins to avoid vital human issues. The most common thing is that we want to make the child first and foremost a specialist for the sake of economic security. But the question is how far we are helping him or her to be an integrated man or woman?

At the age of super-growth of industry and technology, we cannot discard technical knowledge. But, technological progress introduces wider and deeper social, psychological and cultural issues also, which invites misery and destruction. Sometimes, technique without understanding leads to enmity and heartlessness. Most of us are aware of this, but we do not know how to deal with it. We are concerned with principles, methods and ideals. J. Krishnamurti says that education in the true sense helping the individual to be mature and free, to flower greatly in love and goodness; that is what we should be interested in, and not in shaping the child according to some idealistic pattern. So, objective search for facts only should not be the aim of comprehensive education. The goal of education is to help the individual realize his best self. There is a significance of life and education must have the capacity to discover it. If education does not cultivate an integrated outlook of life, life would become a series of conflicts. An individual is a composite being made up of different entities. The function of education is to create an integrated and intelligent human being synthesizing the different entities.

The human personality is a multifaceted and multi-dimensional entity. It has many layers from surface behaviour to inner depths. The human personality has social accomplishment, psychological growth and spiritual progress. Generally, it has three dimensions *viz*., physical, intellectual and spiritual. Education must take care of all these dimensions. To build a great nation, first of all we need physical strength of the inhabitants. Swami Vivekananda used to say to build a new India we need "muscles of iron and nerves of steel". The surest method of education is the concentration of mind; and thus the quest for physical excellence should be there in our education. As body is the basis of all achievements, we should teach our young children to sit properly, to breathe properly and to develop proper eating habits. The aim and objective of all education is to maintain, sustain and develop a healthy mind in a healthy body. Now-a-days the habit of smoking, drinking and drug addiction is fast growing amidst the student community. It may be due to lack of proper education to maintain bodily health. Gandhiji says that true meaning of education is harmonious development of head, heart and hand.

Learning is a never-ending process. Therefore, education should develop the intellectual capacities for learning. In every moment newer and newer dimensions of knowledge are being added. Education should awake us intellectually. To develop self-directed, creative, rational individuals should be the plan of education. Effective education should enable the individual in updating their knowledge and learning skill to keep them fit to the changing environment. Such education will mould the individual as a resource not as a liability to the nation. The intellectual dimension refers to a person's thinking and memory skills. Reading articles, books and journals, exposure to healthy literature and a proper approach to learning help to develop intellectual faculty. If one is given right direction at the primary level itself, it goes a long way in making one intellectually strong. Lessons in concentration and self-discipline play a key role in developing one's intellect.

On the other hand, we should not underestimate the importance of emotional aspect of human personality. Man is the most beautiful combination of thinking, feeling and willing. Now-a-days life is full of stress. Due to emotional imbalance violence, terror, crime neuroses occur in our society. Divisions and subdivisions on the basis of caste, colour, creed, religion, and language are conspicuous in today's society. Therefore, education should address properly the psychological, emotional and aesthetic aspects of human personality. Otherwise, one will lose creativity.

Spirituality is ignored in comparison to other dimensions of human personality in contemporary education. Spiritual development is the need of the hour. It should not be confused with religious education. The main function of education is the development of an all-round and well balanced personality of students. When the emotional, social and spiritual aspects of human personality are not properly developed, the growth of attitudes, habits, values, skills and interest among pupils are hindered. It leads the students sometime towards anxiety, frustration, depression etc.

We cannot think of human life outside society. An individual must care for the whole society where he thinks to be existent. We have a right to live; we also have the obligation to respect life. Our existence cannot be understood abstractly or theoretically. Social virtues like helpfulness, punctuality, cleanliness, teamwork, discipline, dedication should be promoted by education. Both the beginning and end of education should lead to the understanding of life. The understanding of life leads to self-confidence. Only a self-confident individual assumes responsibility for his mistakes and is able to distinguish between what is in his control and what is not.

Only man has the capacity to be aware of beauty, to create beauty and to respond to beauty. He is not a machine. We have no right to mould the child according to a particular pattern, or to determine our own ambitions, hopes and fears. Our intention should be creating human beings who are efficient as well as creative. In the true sense, education always has the aim to make the life a good one to live. It should be at the same time dynamic and futuristic. The growth of industrialization and globalization creates individuals with fragmented personalities. Education must arise to meet this challenge by developing the individuals with self-actualized personalities. Dr. S. Radhakrishnan said that we need today is the education of the whole man—physical, vital, mental, intellectual and spiritual.

10

Women Empowerment: Issues Regarding Power and Powerlessness

Women are integral part of our socio-economic system. Their progress very often reflects the progress of the nation. As we know that in the developing countries women have a low social and economic status, in such countries empowerment of women is essential. Generally, women empowerment means distribution of social power and control of resources in favour of women. The emancipation of women consists of liberation from religious, legal, economic and sexual oppression. Their emancipation is both necessary and desirable as it will provide social justice.

Though the word 'women empowerment' means many things to many people due to ideology or pre-conceived notions it is a holistic concept which includes the following components:

1. Right to have equal access to opportunities for using resources.
2. Right to have choices in matters relating to one's life.
3. Economic independence.
4. Prohibition of gender discrimination.
5. Participation in all decision-making bodies.
6. Freedom from violence.

The Concept of Power

Women empowerment is a matter of redefining women status. The concept of power and authority are implicit in the notion of women empowerment. Power has two central aspects, control over resources (physical, human, intellectual, financial and the self) and control over ideology (beliefs, values and attitudes). Empowerment generates new notion of power, new understanding of power, an experiment with ways of democratizing and sharing power. The empowerment of women results in women having—

(a) power to acquire the ability to make choices;
(b) power within to have agency in seeking higher levels of access and control; and
(c) power with sharing power with men.

Power is the key word of the term empowerment. It is to gain power, to develop power, to take or seize power, to facilitate or enable power and to give grant or permit power. At the same time, it should not be understood that to empower women we have to give women more power to dominate others, to abuse others, to exploit men or to establish any sort of superiority over men. Women empowerment is empowerment of men and women both. To enable them is to identify and improve their hidden talents, abilities, capacity and real identity. Empowerment is not about power but about changing the balance of power, or balance distribution of power between man and women. So, empowerment is—

- **Power within:** individual changes in confidence and consciousness.
- **Power to:** increase in skills, abilities including caring in income.
- **Power over:** changes in power relations within households, communities and at the micro-level.
- **Power with:** organization of the powerless to enhance individual abilities and/or ability to challenge power relations. It is a kind of social change.

The State of Powerlessness

Women lack power and authority in every sphere of life. They experience powerlessness not just in the household but, also in the interaction of multiple social, political and economic institutions. They become easy prey to exploitation and subjugation. Women remain powerless due to their illiteracy, lack of awareness, lack of information and knowledge about markets and skills. Overall, low self-esteem and self-confidence, lack of money and power, and lack of job opportunity make them dependent and vulnerable. Ignorance of one's own rights leads women to subjugation and deprivation. Two significant reasons for subjugation of women in India are not having education and denial of exposure to activities outside homes. There are a number of challenges in the social, economic and political scenario that women face in establishing their rights and equality. The issues, challenges and strategies to empower women have become complex phenomena.

The secondary status of women is a sad social reality, which is common to almost all countries and cultures. Their subordinate position is not only thrust upon them but, also made a part of their minds. The common conception of their supposed inferiority and continuation of their unequal treatment, these two have become permanent hindrances. Cultural factor prevailing in India is over-riding preference for male child by Indian parents. The results are female foeticide and unfavourable sex-ratio. Offences related to marriage include bigamy, adultery, cruelty to life, dowry death and so on.

There are several hardships in the process of women empowerment. There are ideological as well as institutional constraints that women experience in the path of empowerment. The tension between women's empowerment and the potential loss of male privileged is real and does occur. A major set of constraints to women's economic empowerment lies in deep-rooted customs and traditions. Some traditions, customs, rituals, dogmas, beliefs, attitudes, institutions oppress women in family and seize their freedom and right to live with dignity. These factors look down upon women as inferior to men.

Relevant Issues

When we start discussing women empowerment, we will find that it is an active two way process—

- Empowerment that is an externally induced process involving the creation of conditions that enable women to exercise their autonomy.
- Self-empowerment—a process where women find time and

space of their own to begin to re-examine their lives critically and collectively.

But, women in India are trapped by those issues which initiate the conflict of power and powerless. Usually, it is observed that women have chosen the faulty way of living. They themselves have trained their mind and body to lead life of subordination, exploitation and discrimination.

- Women are powerless because of the focus on patriarchal kinship system (without factors).
- Psychological factors which are responsible for prioritizing of women's reproductive and productive roles (within factors).
- Socio-cultural factors condition women's mind. Women perceive themselves as naturally and physically weak.

Besides lack of accessibility to education, some others who get chance to pursue are even facing problems like financial difficulties, resistance from family members, lack of space in the house to pursue independent studies, eve teasing, negative attitude of teachers, harassment by fellow students, diminutive personal interest and so on. Lack of values such as social and family values of mutual love, respect, and understanding, trust of caring and sharing, forgiveness has become eye-catching. It is miserable that women are not considered as worthy human beings. Predominance of inhuman values like violence against women like sexual violence, vulgar sex, rape etc. is aching. Besides these, negative mindset, unhealthy attitude and psyche of man towards girl child and women also reflect scenario of powerlessness.

Patriarchy system leads to discrimination, oppression, exploitation, disregard, insult, violence and control of women freedom. Women occupy lower status in patriarchal society. Indian society is still facing this problem. The happiness of women revolves around their virtues and chastity as daughters, wives mothers and widows. Patriarchal family ideology puts the entire responsibility for domestic work and child care on women. The responsibility is very often disvalued.

A modern woman is more independent in taking decisions and making her own moves exercising her free will. But is she emancipated in the true sense? I, personally realize that her emancipation itself involves further complexities as by-products of much desired liberation. It is ironic that with all external liberties she has become an automation balancing both household and profession. Women in our society are powerless due to above mentioned factors. We should put hands together to empower them. But, once they feel empowered they have to face another state which again forces them to land in a powerless situation.

Women have to work doubly harder to prove themselves. Time pressure for woman is more in comparison to men in the Indian ethos as she has to shoulder several responsibilities as daughter, wife, mother, mother-in-law, grand-mother in addition to being a professional. Each one is equally important to maintain equilibrium in the society. It is tougher for a woman to do the balancing act. For an educated working woman it is a triple burden which includes responsibilities of family, community and office or workplace. A working woman has to be constantly on her toes. Sometimes, family expects a woman to be a super woman who will do everything with utmost sincerity and hard work.

Woman's career is still considered secondary in Indian society. The major section of the society loves to see a woman as a mother or a house-wife. Often a married woman has to forgo her career because the productive academic years coincide with the years of child bearing and rearing. In such situation academic pursuit of woman takes the backstage. A professional woman faces innumerable challenges in keeping balance between career and family. It definitely hampers natural womanly attitudes of love, care, patience, etc. Sometimes she becomes unable to take proper care of her children. It is true that an empowered woman can bring up a child with healthy outlook towards life. But, at the same time it should be realized that she can give her best to society when her needs and aspirations get due respect in her family and society.

It is an open truth that working women have to face problems just by virtue of their being women. Working women here are referred to those who are in paid employment. A gender bias creates an obstacle at the recruitment stage itself. Problems of gender bias weighed down women in the industrial sector. The age-old belief of male superiority over women creates several hurdles for women at their place of work. She has to almost always shoulder the burden of household tasks as well. A woman could still bear up with these problems if she had control over the money she earns. But, in most families even now her salary is handed over to father, husband or in-laws. So, the basic motive for seeking employment of getting independence is nullified in cases of many women.

It is very thorny for working mothers to leave their children at home without proper security and to go to office. They use to leave the children under the care of a servant which gives rise to so many unmanageable problems and mental anxiety. Earning women sometimes cannot give children got good initial primary education. Sometimes, conditions surrounding them at workplace also make them powerless. A study conducted by the Psychology Department of SNDT University, Churchgate, on Mumbai's female workforce provides insights into the psychological problems they face. Dr. H.L. Kaila, Head of the Psychology Department at SNDT, says, "Most of the health problems faced by the city's working women, between the ages of 22 and 58, stem from their workplace. Other psychosomatic problems like backaches, eye problems, fatigue, chest pain, loss of appetite and insomnia are a result of the same." It is absolutely essential that women work and give the financial support is very much needed at almost every home. But, supposed empowered women have been suffering from so many psychosomatic problems and finally become powerless in different aspects of life. The so-called empowerment is forcing women who really want to care for their own children into money making machines and zombies. Consequently, they scream at their underloved husband and children at the moment they step inside the door. It is a common picture that both parents working and not giving enough time and love to their children. Sometimes, it creates an imbalance in the home. Children are turning to drugs, violence and sex because the home is such a miserable place due to a much stressed parents, particularly overly tired mom! So, women empowerment is putting helping hands in increasing divorce rate and even infertility rate.

Most of the problems that inundated working women are in reality rooted in the social perspective of the position of women. Traditionally, men are seen as the breadwinner and women as the house-keepers, child bearers and rearers. This typecast role model continues to put obstacles before the working women. A fundamental change is required in the attitudes of the employers, policy-makers, family members and other relatives and the public at large.

The way out

There is probably no better way of empowering women but through education. Educated women make better mothers and wives than illiterate sisters. Education is not only for them, through education they know essentials of personal; hygiene, nutrition and child care which are essential for the health of her family (husband and children). It is universally acknowledged that knowledge generates self-worth, confidence and self-esteem. Therefore, the sure way to empower women is to educate her. Education is at the centre of all strategies for women's empowerment. It is the key to raise the health status of women and also employment. Education is proved to be the sole significant instrument in improving the status of women. A society can prosper making women educated and empowered. In 20th century education was a means for a woman's empowerment, but today she has the right to education as a citizen.

'Proper education' is not for degree, but for all-round development. It includes physical development, mental development, intellectual development, aesthetic development and spiritual development. "Education is one of the most important means of empowering women with the knowledge, skills and self-confidence necessary to participate fully in the development process." (International Conference, 1994). 'Proper education' must change our attitudes and policies with the objective to give each and every human being (irrespective of sex) greater freedom to make choice about his/her own lives. To revolutionize one's attitude towards life and to remodel one's behaviour-pattern education is the only answer. Education can indeed help girls and women to know their rights and to gain confidence to claim them and this is where empowering women come.

Empowering women should come from within. At the same time, it is true that education could be a good help. In 'proper education' one gets the best education; one becomes sure that he or she knows his or her worth in order to act upon these things. One will try to look at oneself with pride and honour so that he or she will be confident enough to face the world. Confidence is something that no one can give to; it is something that one needs to earn oneself. 'Proper education' should lead to greater self-confidence and ability to control the factors which affect negatively women's lives. It should give them courage to fight against violence, exploitation and injustice with forward looking progressive in their thinking and action. Such education must inculcate better value in both men and women and their children. 'Proper education' should make an individual understand that man and women both must be supportive. Women should not be denied basic social and domestic rights due to gender bias and the empowerment of women and real social development are interrelated. 'Proper education' will enrich both men and women with a better perspective in life which will surely be very beneficial not only to their children but even to those who were around them.

'Proper education' must have the capacity to distinguish between westernization and modernization. It must make clear that women empowerment is not something like drinking, smoking or goes out with friends. No kinds of women day, rallies and *mahila samiti* can help it until and unless we are not changing the way we think and this would be possible only by 'proper education'.

The Indian society is now experiencing drastic change in economy, social structure and family structure. The women in India are enjoying more liberty and equality than before. But, still they have not been restored to the rightful place. The harsh reality is that lots of women have been facing miseries like bride burning, rape, subjugation, and dowry. "Discrimination against women begins at or even before birth" (*Fourth Report on Human Development in Asia: The Gender Question*, Prepared by the Mahbub-ul-Haq Development Centre). The discrimination of women is from womb to tomb. Therefore, our constitution legalizes what our old scriptures prescribe as social duty. The National Policy (2001) was formulated with a view to bridging the gap between the goals enunciated in the constitution, legislation and policies plan, programmes on one hand and situational reality of the status of women in India. It is a balance between power and powerless situation. One should realize that power does not come from any superior biological or physical but from social and economic sources. Women Empowerment is the one of the opportunities. It is the mentality of the people and how are they going to handle the situation.

11

Cultural Globalization: An Observation of Indian Scenario

Globalization is the word used to indicate a set of complex and multifaceted changes that started to take place in the second half of the Twentieth century. As a result of super power rivalry in the period of Cold War, global interdependence came to the surface. Initially, the capabilities and resources of superpowers, spread of international trade, collapse of Communism, technological innovations, Western liberal politics, all these fuelled the process of globalization. And at present, it is an increasing flow of technology, trade, finance, ideas, people and cultures caused by sophisticated technology of communications, travels and neoliberal capitalism.

The term 'globalization' was introduced and popularized by R. Robertson in 1983. Tomlinson defines globalization as complex connectivity, the expansion of social ties across the planet. Globalization is the process of complex interrelationship between states and people. It eliminates geographical distance and territorial boundaries. Arjuna Appadurai (1996) designates this process as the world of flows. Globalization can be portrayed by five different flows. They are—ethnoscapes, mediascapes, technoscapes, financescapes and ideoscapes. Ethnoscapes refers to the movement of people in the form of immigrants, refugees, exiles, migrant workers, business travellers, tourists, knowledge workers and so on. Mediascapes leads to the dispersal of information and images through computer, television, radio, newspaper, and journal etc. Technoscapes implies a flow of technologies and mechanical information from one place to another. Financescapes indicates flow of money and capital through banking system, stock exchanges, foreign investments and markets. Ideoscapes means the flow of knowledge, ideas and ideologies. At present, globalization has become such a powerful force which persuades restructuring at three basic levels—

(i) Changes in economic life.
(ii) Changes in power and politics.
(iii) Changes in knowledge, culture and identity.

Globalization is not simply synonym for global business; it is much more than that. It also involves the process of extension of human activities, relations and networks across the globe. 'The local' and 'the national' become subordinate to 'the global'. People's ideas, acts and behaviour, as a whole the way of life and cultures across the globe have witnessed the transformation due to the revolutionary changes in the field of technology, transport and communication. Fraser has rightly commented that globalization is a word on every commentator's lips now-a-days, but is very difficult to define satisfactorily, for it arises in so many different contexts like economic, sociological, political, cultural and environmental.

The significant dimensions of globalization are—economic, political and cultural globalization. Most commonly, cultural globalization is a significant dimension of globalization which creates global culture. It is hegemonic in nature. Cultural globalization persuades a worldview towards intercultural exchange and promotes a multicultural society. Such a society has due respect to local and regional cultures. Cultural globalization refers to the transmission of ideas and values around the world. It extends and intensifies social relations. It promotes the formation of shared norms, customs, rules and knowledge. These shared standards encourage people to associate their individual and collective cultural identities. Gradually, interconnectedness among different populations and cultures is increasing. Cultural globalization brings about human integration and hybridization. Multiculturalism and cosmopolitanism are to some extent manifestations of cultural globalization.

Global communication makes the world a global village. As a result of application of modern communications, different societies come closer and contact between cultures is increasing. Cultural globalization acts as key force that keeps cultural traditions alive. Promotion of local culture is quite easier with the process of globalization. One can be aware of cultural diversities of different parts of the world and of different communities. But there are both pros and cons of cultural globalization.

Cultural globalization provides better understanding of values and attitudes of different communities across the globe. It proves itself a strong means to lessen misconceptions about other people and cultures. It has made access to new cultural products, like art, entertainment, institutions etc. Capacity to communicate and defend one's values and ideals globally, instant access to information from anywhere in the world, customization or adaptation of global cultural trends to local environment are some other positive aspects of cultural globalization. On the other hand, cultural globalization carries the dangers of cultural homogenization, cultural imperialism or cultural colonialism. Spread of commodity-based consumer culture is the most harmful effect of cultural globalization. Westernization gallops in such a pace that it gulps down the distinctive features of some small cultures. Moreover, cultural globalization has become very active in spreading dangerous or violent ideals.

Culture and traditions of any geographic region always has its uniqueness. These are the distinguishing factors for a population within a geographic boundary. India is famous for its cultural diversity. Its unique civilization has no parallel in the world. Various groups of people with different racial, ethnic, linguistic, regional, religious and cultural backgrounds populate it. History illustrates that India has never been free from external linkage. It is conspicuous that immigration and migration played a very crucial role in structuring and restructuring Indian society and culture. Since 19th century onwards, socio-cultural changes under the modern West's impact have considerably started in India. The British rule and later Euro-American influence have initiated the globalization process in Indian society. The uniqueness of Indian culture has been influenced to the varying degrees in the name of globalization.

There are distinctions between individualistic Western culture and collectivistic Indian culture. Therefore, the impact of cultural globalization on various segments of Indian culture presents a complex picture producing both positive and negative results. Cultural globalization has resulted in a major transformation of the lifestyle and living standard of people. Globalization has not only inculcated the Westernization in India, but conversely the Indian culture has also spread its impact globally. Indian cuisine is one of the most popular cuisines across the globe. Indian classical music has gained worldwide recognition. Western music is becoming very popular in our country. Fusing Indian music along with Western music is encouraged among musicians. Now-a-days, Indian dance shows are held globally. The number of foreigners who are eager to learn *Bharatanattyam* is rising. Western dance forms such as Jazz, Hip hop, Salsa, Balley have become popular among Indian youngsters.

It is observed in current Indian society that through globalization, men and women are gaining equal right to education, to earn, and to speak. Women have gained certain opportunities for job options and women's rights get reorganization as a part of the human rights. Their empowerment has given considerable opportunities and possibilities of improving employment conditions through global solidarity and co-ordination. It is found that the growth of computer and other technologies enabled women with better wages, flex timings, and capacity to negotiate their role and status in home and at corporate level.

On the other hand, nuclear families are emerging. The joint families have become strange to the Indians especially to those residing in the urban areas or in the small flat of metropolitan cities. Consequently, the nuclear families have lost the patience to get adjusted into the joint family. The ego factor that has got penetration into the mind of Indian youth is undoubtedly a product of globalization. Marriage, which is used to be considered birth after birth, as bonding of the soul's, is becoming a professional bond today or a so-called commitment to share life without compromising their self-interests. Earlier, for ages in Indian culture and society, both the genders were kept at a distance, with many restrictions and limitations to the approach. With the emergence of globalization and Western culture, youth have started mixing up well with each other. The friendly approach and the socializing feature are appreciable. But, the total breakout of restrictions has infected the Indian mindset. This has given birth to new relationships like living together, playing up with the physical relationship etc. The increased cases of rape and sexual abuse are the result of the perverted mind and again the perversion is imported by such values very much alien to our mother culture.

Employment through MNCs has become profitable deals and attracts the bulk of energetic youth of India. But they are working for the other countries as their customer care representatives. Due to economic slavery to these MNCs, a huge portion of manpower is losing health and status hankering after money. It impacts age-old culture of India. Every bit of a person's way of living, i.e. food habit, taste, fashion, commodities etc. has changed. It is true that globalization increases a country's material prosperity but it comes with a high cultural cost.

Right now, the privileged class of Indian society is able to use the opportunities and benefits of globalization. People are passionate for new machines, new equipments, new gadgets, new buildings, new cars, new dresses and even new drugs. Various terrible things are taking place in the name of globalization, such as theft, drugs, narcotics etc. As a result, some Indian people are becoming more materialistic, pragmatic and money minded. This section of society is becoming more loyal to Western culture. But another picture is also observed. Besides *namaste* 'Hi', 'Hello' is used to greet people. Festivals of Western culture like Valentine's Day Friendship Day, Kiss Day, Hug Day, Fathers' Day, Mothers' Day etc. are spreading across India. In the same way, *Yoga* of Indian culture is recognized and practiced widely in Western countries. The great *mantra* of non-violence is spread worldwide. The motto *Vasudhaiva kutumbakam,* i.e. we are all human family is a gift of Indian culture to bind all humans.

Intellectuals, NGOs, Government officials and different national and International organizations are studying the impact of globalization on various aspects of life in India including its impact on Indian culture, value system and employment. But, let me present my own observations in this regard—

(i) More access to information and technology transforms our lifestyle with innumerable physical and material benefits.

(ii) Greater cultural exchange caused by cultural globalization is increasing tolerance and understanding among people.

(iii) Society has become more open compared to its earlier conservative look due to exposure to other cultures.

(iv) Social changes contributed by global worldview as gender equality, women empowerment, greater respect for human rights, environmental awareness, conservation of natural resources etc. have revolutionized the mindset of people.

(v) Globalization, with its cultural dimension has liberalized our attitudes, reduced our biases and predispositions about people, situations and communities worldwide.

(vi) Cultural globalization is very often blamed for increasing risk behaviours such as smoking and alcohol consumption, increasing social conflict, loss of identity, dislocation and dissatisfaction. It is also accused harshly for spreading Westernized consumer culture.

(vii) Though cultural globalization claims to support diversity, but it is promoting a worldwide monoculture—the Westernization.

(viii) Cultural globalization indirectly props up lust, jealousy, hatred and unhealthy competition.

(ix) In the geographical sense, Colonial Empire came to an end, but exploitation in the name of cultural globalization still exists.

Globalization has a huge impact on cultural, social, monetary, political, and communal life of a country like our India. It is identified as a dominant ideology. It has left back its footprints at every sphere of life. No doubt, globalization is a key word to understand and examine social complexity and recent changes of our society. But culture should not be treated as commodity. It should be a way of exploring good life. Connectivity and interdependence among cultures across national borders should be capitalized for better future of human race.

12
Revisiting Family Values

Most commonly, family is the minimal unit of a society. It is to which we all belong and from where our identity comes. Family is important to everyone in the world. We all belong to a particular family and it is our family that keeps us together. Family is a bond, a long lasting relationship. It is through a family that we learn the values of love, trust, hope, belief, cultures, morals and traditions. Without having a family, no person is complete and the completeness comes with good family bonding. A person is valued based on his family and upbringing. Truly speaking, family is like a safe harbour, where we feel secure.

Each person has a different and unique concept of family in his heart. The strong role which family plays, family's communication, and its supports are the three main reasons that make family so important. To me family is that or those members who support and care for me. They watch out for me and are there when I need them. They also help me reach goals that I set for myself. The dictionary explains family as a fundamental social group consisting of one or two parents and the children they raise. Human species is the most powerful species on the earth, but at the same time it is also the weakest species. If a human child is allowed to survive of its own, it just cannot survive. So, the support of family is extreme necessity for the growth of every human child.

On the other hand, a value could be defined as an attitude that one wants to keep as a standard for judging himself and the rest of the world. It is the basis for his sense of right and wrong, good and bad. It is our values that drive us to act in certain ways, to lead a certain lifestyle. If family and value-sense are viewed intimately then it will lead to a philosophy that how one wants to live his family life. In a family each member is expected to behave in a particular order. Family values mean a traditional set of social standards defined by the family and customs which provide the emotional and physical basis for raising a family. It is expected that the members of the family divide their work in a way that all members perform complementary functions. The human child gets the first lesson of conduct from parents. The values a family develops are traditionally the foundation for how children learn, grow and function in the world. Traditional family values usually include topics such as religion, marriage, communication, traditions, morals, holidays, interactions with relatives and how time is spent together. They are usually passed on from one generation to the next, giving children the structure and boundaries in which to function and bloom. Family time, love, play and work give children this foundation. Principles which are lovingly set, explained, and implemented—provide children with security. Values are to show the desire to have a good, orderly family in which the members care for one another.

Obviously, if we value our family we will defend it from external forces. The only sure guard is the placing value high. If we value our spouse, we will respect his or her opinions and views. If we value our children, we will protect them from assault, abuse and abandonment. If we value our dignity as a woman or man, we will avoid shameless acts and work towards making it honourable. If we value our life, we will not try to destroy it by taking intoxicating things. Once people begin to show respect for values in their cultural, educational, family and social system our society will be a better place to live without any fear of insecurity. The love within a family teaches a child about solidarity, which brings the teachings of virtue, sensitivity and assertiveness. Everyone has the need to feel loved, but the best love there can be is the love of a family.

Family values became a popular political term in the late Twentieth century. Familialism is the ideology that promotes the family and its values as an institution. The phrase has different meanings in different cultures. In the late 20th and early 21st Centuries, the term has been frequently used in political debate, especially by social and religious conservatives, who believe that the world has seen a decline in family values since the end of the Second World War. But, all these 'isms' and debates are nothing other than political catchphrases. Actually, family values are a set of beliefs or morals that help maintaining family unity and social interaction as well as providing for a societal view for childhood development. They are basically the core of our way of living. They have been important since the very beginning of our civilization. The principles, laws and rules in one's own family may be different from others, but the principles behind them should be the same; like simplicity, consistency, penalty, and a provision for regret to avoid the penalty.

Family values have brought considerable amounts of happiness to us throughout the course of our history. So, let us take the time to share family values and traditions with our children, schedule family meetings together, share meals together where the family gets together to talk about the day, schedule recreation and relaxation into day-to-day life, work together within the family to identify and create our own family values. Family meeting is extremely necessary to determine family values. Family meetings provide an opportunity for all members to come together and share their thoughts, perspectives and their lives. A family meeting is an opportunity to give priority to those things the family values and establish traditions. Things such as how one views marriage and commitment, what role religion or spirituality plays in a family, how emotionally available a particular individual to others, his beliefs about sharing responsibility, the common interests shared by spouse and family, hobbies and how family time is spent, how family decisions are made, how family traditions are established, and so on should be good topics to discuss at a family meeting to help determine how these things are valued. Family principles need regular discussion and recommitment. Setting them up in the first place needs to be a highly communicative process. Kids need to understand that the purposes of these principles are safety and happiness. Then only they show an increase of trust and love.

Work, play and love are described as the three usual basic household tasks. There are many activities that fall under these categories and all of them are important. Sometimes, we get caught-up in work and other related activities and neglect play and love. No doubt, now-a-days we all are extremely busy for self-centric interests. People are more diversified and separated in their ways. It is discussed that the place of values in our society today is in a jumble; most especially our family values are in a complete shuffle. We often work hard because we are invested in our career goals, material things and financial rewards. But, bonding does not happen overnight. We cannot buy or demand it. We all have realized that without a balanced life of incorporating play and having loving relationships, our lives become stressful, upsetting and unsatisfying.

We all know that literacy, health and nutritional status and level of income evaluate the current status of human development; but to evaluate the spiritual dimension of human development parameters should be based on values. Where would we be without love and compassion? All people desire family values, such as love, care, intimacy, acceptance, commitment, and shared responsibility. A person who is called successful in life is a person who has a happy family. What we value we must respect, what we value we must defend, what we value we must protect.

Life and people are always changing, but the main values and bases of the concept of family should always remain present. We expect that the interest of each member of the family should be protected; and love and trust alone govern the management of a family. As the parents do not seek any personal benefit when they try to give something to their children, the children too should recognize the contributions made by the parents in building their lives. They should pass on the same benefits to their own children and take care of their parents when they grow old. When families successfully care for their members honouring family values they make an inestimable contribution to the large society.

13

Dharma and Present Day Society

Commonly, the idea of *dharma* refers to the general moral sense possessed only by man which gives meaningfulness to human life. *Dharma* is the authoritative *puruṣārtha* in Indian value-scheme. All modes of human activity derive their meaning and significance only when integrated into a meaningful pattern, which is *dharma*. "It (*dharma*) is very difficult to understand by an ordinary person. Yet, it is within the heart of every person."[1] Metaphysically, *dharma* signifies the essential nature of a thing. *Dharma* is really the inner law of being. For example, *dharma* of fire is heat, *dharma* of water is coolness, and the *dharma* of warrior is to fight. In common parlance, *dharma* means right way of living, proper conduct, path of righteousness, faith and duty. Broadly speaking, *dharma* has been used in three different senses: (i) it stands for the moral law conceived as constituting the eternal moral order of the universe; (ii) the principle of duty; and (iii) satisfaction of sensuous desires (*kāmya-karma*).

Though in the narrower sense *dharma* means performance of rituals and ceremonies, it has a general meaning designing moral excellence. The term *Dharma* is variously translated as Religion, Virtue, Law, and Duty. All these words convey something of the meaning, but to use anyone of them as an equivalent is highly misleading....In India in those days no clear distinction was drawn between moral and religious duties, usages, customary observance and law, and *dharma* was the term which was applied to whole complex of forms of conduct that were settled or established.[2]

Etymologically, *dharma* means "that which supports" right activity or duty, i.e. activity which is the result of a goodwill. The word *dharma* is derived from the root *dhṛ*. The Sanskrit term *dharma* signifies the underlying order in nature and life (human or other) considered to be in accord with that order. It is usually understood as the principle or law which sustains, supports or maintains (*dhārayati*) the individual as well as the social order. With respect to spirituality, *dharma* might be considered the way of the Higher Truth. *Dharma* is an omnibus term which does not have any adequate translation in English. As there is no precise Western equivalent to translate *Dharma*, Austin B. Creel describes *dharma* as the pattern of ethical regulation and justification of that pattern. *Dharma* refers to what one should do and why one should do so.[3] He adds that *dharma* has naturalistic and normative aspects. Normative aspect of *dharma* is the religious and moral law. The naturalistic aspect is *dharma* as an attitude, a disposition. Karl Potter describes *dharma* as the attitude of concern towards others as a fundamental extension of the self.

T.M.P. Mahadevan says, "*Dharma* consists in leading a life of duty, living in harmony and peace, with development of character and refinement of soul."[4] *Dharma* is a regulative principle, which should govern all our activities and pursuits. *Dharma* is the inner reality that makes a thing what it is. For example, it is the *dharma* of the bee to make honey. It is a thing's essence. Radhakrishnan in his *Religion and Society* talks of *dharma* as the norms which sustain the universe, the principles of a thing by virtue of which it is what it is. *Dharma* is said to be possessed of a positive and a negative significance. It is positive as it guides the man of determined will to lead a life of worth. In negative aspect, it demonstrates a check on the course of the erring man to take him to the right path. In Hindu thought, the term *dharma* has been used in two senses: the principle in accordance with which all human actions ought to be performed and the various duties to be discharged in various spheres of life. Professor Somló names *dharma* as the 'primitive first norm' in which law, religion, ethics and convention cannot clearly be distinguished. But, G. Mess interprets that instead of 'primitive first norm' 'primeval norm' would be more fitting.

Sometimes, *Dharma* is found as a mythological personage, a *deva* or a divine being in charge of *dharma*. In the *Bhāgavata Purāṇa, dharma* is mentioned as the father of the fourth *avatāra* or divine incarnation.[5] *Dharma* was created by Brahmā from his right breast in the human form for the sake of production of human beings. He is married to daughters of Dakṣa. *Dharma* was the father of

Śama, Kāma and *Harṣa. Purāṇic* tradition expresses that Dakṣa, the son of Prajāpati gave away his thirteen daughters as wives to *Dharma*. They are *Śraddhā* (faith), *Maitrī* (friendliless), *Dayā* (compassion), *Śānti* (peace), *Tuṣṭi* (contentment), *Puṣṭi* (maintenance), *Kriyā* (action), *Unnati* (promotion), *Buddhi* (mind), *Medhā* (sharp-mind), *Titikṣā* (forbearance), *Hrī* (meekness) and *Mūrti* (manifestation).[6] It appears that one of the key meanings of *dharma* is moral virtue or moral practice.

After all, "We cannot reduce the meanings of *dharma* to one general principle; nor is there one single translation which would cover all its usages."[7] *Dharma* is equated with moral conscience. The *Mahābhārata* mentions eight types of *dharma* such as sacrifice, study of the *śāstras*, gift, austerity, truthfulness, forgiveness, self-control and non-greed. The popular sense of *dharma* is right action. *Dharma* maintains (*dhṛ*) the world (*loka*). It sustains all people (*prajā*). *Dharma* is the supporter of the whole universe (*jagat*), therefore, it is called the highest. It is the moral law which makes orderly society possible. From another aspect, *dharma* is explained in the *Mahābhārata* as making violent beings non-violent. Again, in the *Śāntiparva*, it is described that *ahiṁsā* is the cause of *dharma*; what is done through non-violence is of a permanent nature. The Jaina view which pays attention to the non-injury of all living beings is also on the same line. *Dharma* implies concern for all existing being in the universe. But, they (Jainas) add that excessive sexual enjoyment destroys *dharma*.

Dharma or good action is that which leads to *iṣṭa* or desirable. Good action leads to the fulfillment of proper desire. Moral action is a cause of pleasure (*harṣa*).[8] One gets great fame (*mahat-yasas*) by following *dharma*.[9] Sometimes, *dharma* is described as merit. Merit acquired by virtues may protect one on all sides. It is a sort of armour (*kavaca*) or a protection against demons. Even the god of death protects one who is established in *dharma*. One who is pleased to hear, see, perform or speak about *dharma* is purified by the acquire merit.[10]

One practising social custom or *sadācāra* achieve long life, wealth, sons, happiness, permanent abode of god and respect from learned people.[11] According to Jainism, action performed by rightness, including right verbal knowledge, and control of evil motives bring forth merits (*puṇṇa*). According to *Dhammapada*, sin increases if one is unmindful and does not behave morally. It is only the pure *sīla* (moral conduct) which is instrumental to happiness.

Kumārila Bhaṭṭa's *Ślokavārttika* expresses "the *Veda* is the means of arriving at the right notion of *dharma*."[12] In the *Ṛg-Veda*, the first concept that is strikingly *dhārmic* is that of *Ṛta*. It is considered that the Vedic cosmic principle of *Ṛta* is the foundation of morality. Literally, it means "the course of things". A.A. MacDonell points out *Ṛta* as "order in the moral world as truth and 'right' and in the religious world as sacrifice or 'rite'."[13] The intent of the Vedic texts was to teach *dharma* or duty through injunctions and prohibitions. In the *Ṛg-Veda*, *dharma* signifies upholder or supporter. According to the *Atharvaveda*, *dharma* means the principle or the substance which can sustain any object.

On the eve of the *Mahābhārata* war, sage Veda Vyāsa cried and cried: "I cry with arm uplifted, yet none heedeth. From righteousness follow forth abundantly both Pleasure and Profit. Why then do you not follow Righteousness?" *Dharma* (virtue), *artha* (wealth) and *kāma* (pleasure) constitute the complete good of man. "When one's possession and passion are regulated by *dharma*, they are not only conducive to the individual's spiritual progress but also to the realization of the Social Good".[14] By conferring ethical orientation to the impulsive ingredients of human nature, the individual will definitely become ready to view life not from his own narrow angle, but from a broad and wider standpoint. *Dharma* was explicitly defined in terms of certain duties and obligations which were codified in the great law books to maintain the social order. Individual, society and nation can prosper following the path of *dharma* (in the sense of moral virtue, duties and code of conduct). In all stages of human life, either as a student or as a householder, as a forest dweller or an ascetic, *dharma* has to be accepted as paramount. The entire day-to-day life of *puruṣa* (individual) is governed by *dharma*. Though, the impression made by the *śāstric* tradition regarding *dharma* was deep-seated, it refers to a whole way of life rather than to mere doctrines or moral teachings alone. It is very relevant to our social concerns. The happy life is thought to be virtuous. "He is said to know what morality or righteousness is, who is always the friend of all creatures and who is always engaged in the good of all creatures in thought, word and deed".[15]

Some modern thinkers have the tendency to brush away the influence of the *dharma* putting the opinion that it is only disciplines of rituals and religiosity and they bear no meaning in present time. But *dharma* sets out the principles and goals of human behaviour to ensure realization of optimum welfare of both individual and social levels. It is a middle principle between unwarranted pleasure seeking life or attitude and freedom from all unnecessary severity. There are other modern thinkers whose treatments regarding *dharma* are novel. For example, U.N. Ghosal combines *dharma* with law and duty. A.L. Basham examines *dharma* from its cultural standpoint. Dr. B. Khan observes *dharma* from ethical viewpoint. Again, Charles Drekmeir in *Kingship and Community in Early India* analyzed *dharma* as a value legitimized the use of power in ancient India.

There are several instances that Indian traditions have been preserved without a breakdown to the present-day, as for example, the *varṇa dharma*. Even today, it sheds light on a new direction towards social responsibility and stability. Unfortunately, *varṇa* system had been degraded into caste system giving birth to social evil like untouchables. But, if we consider *varṇa* as class, no class is less essential. On the basis of this system, the faculties, the talents, aptitudes and skills were perpetually promoted. Again, the spirit of *āśrama dharma* is still adhered to. In today's society, the division of social classes still exists in another appearance grouped into four social classes: the upper class, the middle class, the working class and the underclass. No doubt, this method of classification is based on wealth occupation. The upper class consists of the rich and wealthy who are able to enjoy a much higher living standard than the rest of the community. The middle class consists of white-collar professionals like lawyers, doctors and teachers who enjoy a reasonable standard of living. The working class is mainly made up of workers in factories and industries, who cannot survive without a salary and own few properties. The underclass is mainly the poor and unemployed, who are dependent on the country to provide them the basic needs of life.

In ancient India, the idea of kingship, ruler-ruled relationship, the interrelationship between the subjects are all controlled and directed by *dharma*. In modern time, justice, equality, human rights etc. are new terms and looks on the face of righteousness. Instead of ancient king, new term 'government' comes to the scene. All the duties and responsibilities of ancient king or state head are in this or that form existing in terms of acts and policies of government. Leaders of political parties, executive head of the state, administrative and judicial officers are bound to do their duties or follow right ways to discharge their responsibilities for smooth progress of the country. On the other hand, if a government turns its back to war would definitely gain prosperity in terms of peace and well-being. This situation cannot be termed as ancient or modern. Now-a-days, it becomes just an evolution that to resolve conflicts by negotiation and non-violent techniques will build a spiritually strong nation. Ruler ought to rule his country following the principle of righteousness. Earnest and careful performance of stately duties obviously develops parent-children relations between rulers and subjects. Kauṭilya's *Arthaśāstra* declares that ideal king regards the happiness of his subjects as his own happiness which can be realized only through the practice of *dharma*. The *Mahābhārata* gives right to the people to resist a bad ruler. It says, "The king who failed to give protection should be abandoned like a split boat at sea."[16]

The *Bṛhadāraṇyaka Upaniṣad* says that there is nothing higher than *dharma*. Henceforth, even a weak man rules a stronger with the help of *dharma*. According to Manu, *dharma* is dynamic and flexible. Mahatma Gandhi declares that politics without morality is a sin. His inspiration of *Rāmarājya* comes from the feature that *Rāma* is the embodiment of *dharma*. Social stability, justice, welfare, harmony, integration, well-being etc. are just other names for *dharma*. Gandhi puts human happiness combined with full mental and moral development as the goal of life. One can be effectively modern and materialist, but at the same time if he cares for his people, he can also be *dhārmic*. Even today, king or the ruler is assumed to be responsible for the maintenance of the moral order or *dharma* in the country. No matter what era, what state it is, the governance process must be just, fair and citizen caring.

In the modern world, carried away by the mechanical way of living people do not think about *dharma*, understand *dharma* and live according to *dharma* just as they do not care for Nature, Culture and Art. It is the root cause for all the problems we are facing and suffering today. *Dharma* is not an old fashioned religious tradition or blind belief based on caste just as human culture is also believed to be. But, on the contrary, it is a reality that people who live according to *dharma*, never fail in anything in the world. Person of *dharma* realizes the Self, understands one's nature, develops it with education and trainings to the best one can, does all works as perfectly as possible with a broad ambition and lives a full life with success in the world. That is why *dharma* is very important and necessary for everyone to follow one's *dharma* in life. The role of *dharma* in current social problems therefore appears to be threefold:

(i) to eliminate the mental ruining that cause us to do wrong, so that we do not add to the problems and suffering in our society;
(ii) to help us bear the stress of competitiveness, crowded or polluted environments; and
(iii) to give us strength to serve and improve our society.

At present, corruptions, material prosperity by dishonest means, lying, stealing, exploitation, crimes of all kind are increasing rapidly. People are divided in the name of caste, community and religion and it is causing serious threat to national integration. All these are result of abandoning the right path, i.e. the path of *dharma*. Today's world has made tremendous progress in science and technology. Lots of amenities and facilities make man's life more and more comfortable. But, the scientific inventions which are useful for constructive activities are being used for destructive terrorist activities. Even man-made sufferings are on the increase as individuals are subjecting other individuals to untold misery and pain by upholding evil actions for selfish ends. Human beings are acting inhumanly using every type of modern scientific knowledge. Everyday newspapers and other media carry news of such atrocities.

Dharma acts as an internal check, a preventive against immoral actions. The desire (*kāma*) and wealth (*artha*) must be rejected if contrary to *dharma*. One can define *dharma* as a scientific path of self-introspection and wisdom. Every individual should regulate his mind, speech and action by constant effort so that he does not inflict any physical and mental injury to other individuals. Manu advocates control of senses (*indriyanigrahaḥ*) as one of ten *Sādhāraṇa dharmas*. *Dharma* laid down a code of conduct covering every aspect of human behaviour. The observance of such regulations is considered a necessity to maintain peace and happiness of individuals and society. *Dharma* should not be destroyed so that we may not be destroyed as a consequence thereof.[17] An orderly society would be in existence if everyone acts according to *dharma*. Such a society can protect the rights of individual. Now, it is the time for resurrection of *dharma*. Multi anti-social activities increase rapidly. If *dharma* is properly preserved, it protects man, society and the universe.

All our present day problems are direct results of disregarding *dharma*. Now-a-days, man pampers wrong actions on account of greed and being actuated by one or more of the six enemies—such as *Kāma* (lust), *Krodha* (anger), *Lobha* (covetousness), *Moha* (delusion), *Mada* (pride), and *Mātsarya* (jealousy). Man becomes corrupt to acquire more money, commits sexual offences against women like rape, adultery, infidelity etc. Rightfully earned money gives mental happiness. So, having secured wealth rightly one must spend the money on the right cause; not in drinking alcohol, immoral sex, giving trouble to others etc.

India is suffering from the fever of controversies among different religious sects. Erosion of value is conspicuous due to the lack of *dharma* in different rituals of religious sects. In general, people wrongly confuse *dharma* with ritualistic religion. To translate *dharma* to the word religion is an unhappy rendering. The result of equating *dharma* with religion in India has been devastating. *Dharma* stands for a way, a path of life rather than for the theology and institutions.

In the social context, Supreme Court of India has also declared *dharma* as that which upholds or supports the stability of the society, maintains the social order and secures the general well-being and progress of mankind. *Dharma* has been conceived as relatives to human needs, orders, and temperaments of man spatial as well as temporal conditions of society. Human good lies in the harmony of the three—desire (*kāma*) wealth (*artha*) and righteousness (*dharma*). B. Kuppuswamy also observes that *dharma* has been one of the most powerful and influential terms in Indian thought and society for millennia, right from the Vedic time up to today. All cannot be great. But, every individual can afford to be good.

Notes

1. *Rāmāyaṇa*, IV. 18.
2. Mckenzie, J., *A Manual of Ethics*, pp. 38-39.

3. Creel, A.B., "*Dharma* as an Ethical Category to Freedom and Responsibility. *Philosophy East and West,* Vol. 22, p. 155.
4. Mahadevan, T.M.P., *Outlines of Hinduism*, p. 6.
5. *Bhāgavata Purāṇa*, 1.3.9.
6. *Ibid.*, 4.1.49-50.
7. Halbfass, W., *Tradition and Reflection: Exploration in Indian Thought,* p. 333.
8. *Carakasaṁhitā,* 2. 41.
9. *Mahābhārata, Bhīṣmaparva*, 65. 17.
10. *Vṛddhagautama Smṛti,* 29.
11. *Parāśarasmṛti*, 6.206 and 208.
12. Jha, G. (tr.) Kumārila Bhaṭṭa, *Ślokavārttika*, p. 555.
13. MacDonell, A.A., *Vedic Mythology*, p. 11.
14. Kane, P.V., *History of Dharma Śāstra,* Vol. 1, p. 1.
15. Reyna, R., *Dictionary of Oriental Philosophy*, Vol. I.
16. *Mahābhārata*, 12.110.11./12.109.14.
17. *Manusaṁhitā,* VI.11-15.

Section III

Reflections on Living Thoughts

14

Gandhi's Non-Violent State: The Ideal and the Actual

Being a revolutionary, Gandhi has put a stateless society as his ideal. He is opposed to the state because the state, according to him, is an instrument of violence. In his view, the state represents violence in a concentrated and organized form. The individual has a soul, but as the state is a soul-less machine. In the ideal state, as conceived by Gandhi, each individual will be a law unto himself and hence, there would be no necessity of a state or state-made law. Gandhi gives us a picture of his best ideal—"Non-violent state". The main characteristics of the Non-violent state are:

(i) There would be minimum use of coercion in it. Police force, with arms; cannot be eliminated. But the police will not be masters of the people. The police in Non-violent state are basically social workers.

(ii) In dealing with crime, the object of the Non-violent state will be neither retribution nor deterrence. Punishment becomes necessary in some cases of crime. But it will be corrective and reformative and not vindictive.

(iii) So far as jails and courts are concerned, jails will be more for reforming the prisoners rather than frightening or breaking them. Prisoners will be treated as defectives and not as criminals to be looked down upon. The jail officials will be their mends and instructors. Judicial work will be done by the Panchayats.

(iv) In the sphere of administration, decentralization will be the keynote of the Non-violent state. Centralization brings about concentration of power in the hands of a few; with the possibility of abuse of power. Non-violent state will be a decentralized society with pervading equality in every sphere of life.

(v) Through decentralization the functions of the state will be gradually reduced and transferred to voluntary associations. In performing its functions, the object of the state will be to serve the masses, and the voluntary organizations will be more effective in this as their aim is more 'service of the people' than acquisition and retention of power.

Ideally Non-violent state is an ordered anarchy. Indeed, it is a contradiction in terms. Ultimately, when non-violence is the governing principle of society, we could not call it a state—it could only be called a non-violent stateless society. And that is the ideal for Gandhi. In such a society, people would simply grow accustomed spontaneously to observe their social obligations without the operation of the state. The necessity of legal enforcement arises because of human imperfections. The more the individuals have imbibed the spirit of non-violence, the less the necessity of the state. The Non-violent state is composed of small self-governing and relatively self-sufficient village communities relying largely on moral and social pressure. This is the implication of Gandhi's concept of *Swarāj*.

In Gandhi's view decentralization was the key to world peace. He began with village *swarāj* and ended up in proposing *Rāmarāja* (enlightened anarchy) through the instrumentality of non-violence. Gandhi was in search of an ideal state where everyone is his own ruler without much interference by the state. When he was asked about the ideal State, he talked about *Rāma Rājya*. By using the *Rāma Rājya* slogan, Gandhi implied an ideal *Rājya* where values of justice, equality, idealism, renunciation and sacrifice are practised. The *Rāmāyaṇa,* in the chapter on *Ayodhyā* gives a majestic description of *Rāma Rājya*, where peace, prosperity and tranquility reigned. *Ayodhyā* literally means "the land without wars". Hence *Rāma Rājya* is described as an ideal state. Obviously in this ideal society everybody follows a code of righteous living and more or less happy, meeting all their essential needs. Gandhi, on *Rāma Rājya*, wrote on February 26, 1947, "Let no one commit the mistake of thinking that

Rāmarājya means a rule of Hindus. My *Rāma* is another name for *Khudā* or God. I want *Khudā Rāj* which is the same thing as the *Kingdom of God on Earth*."

People failed to understand what Gandhi meant by *Rāmarājya*. By *Rāmarājya* he means a divine *Rāj*. Gandhi's faith in God is unshakable. His God was not a personal God. *Rāma,* for him, the almighty God was a guide to noble action. The *Rāmarājya* was promoting an ideal social order where an ideal ruler ruled over his subjects without any distinction whatsoever. Truth, *Dharma* and Justice would be the dominant characteristics of such a society. There was much in common, if one can stretch it between Plato's Ideal Republic and Gandhi's *Rāmarājya*. Gandhi calls *Rāmarājya* as the *Dharmarājya*, the rule of *dharma*. Here, rights accrue automatically from the performance of one's duties. The right to perform one's duty is the only right worth living for. His *Rāmarājya* was not a utopia where idealism alone would reign. It is predominantly a non-violent state which is a practical possibility. "Welfare of all" (*Sarvodaya*), the ideal of *Rāmarājya* depends on the moral conviction of the members.

Gandhi's great concern for all the oppressed and depressed made him unquestioned 20th century prophet. He looked at social welfare in his own unique way. He considered man superior to the system he propounds. '*Sarvodaya*', the greatest good of all through truth and non-violence became the ultimate goal of Gandhi in social welfare. Gandhi made every effort to build the edifice of social reconstruction for '*Sarvodaya*' on the two rock-like pillars of Truth and Non-violence. Gandhi's philosophy of *Sarvodaya* is opposed to any ism of majority, concept of class racial struggle and the principle of greatest good of greatest numbers. Being an apostle of non-violence, Gandhi was repelled by the coercive character of the state. He desired a classless society and partyless democracy. For *Swaraj, Sarvodaya* is necessary. *Sarvodaya* is hostile to the state; there is no space of politics of power. Universalization of self-government is promoted by *Sarvodaya.* It is a powerful intellectual attempt to build a plan of political and social reconstruction.

Nevertheless, Gandhi advocated for a minimal level of state organization to fund some education programmes and to promote his economic concept of trusteeship. Hence, Gandhi was a compromising anarchist. *Swarāj* warrants a stateless society. Adopting *Swarāj* means implementing a system whereby state machinery is virtually zero and the real power directly resides in the hands of people. Dr. Gopinath Dhawan placed Gandhi as a 'philosophical anarchist' because he believed that the '*Sarvodaya*' (the greatest good of all) can be realized only in the classless, stateless democracy. A Non-violent state is committed to *Sarvodaya*, the uplift of all individuals rather than a ruling class or favoured few.

Gandhi was not concerned with constructing a system of philosophy, but mainly with applying the ideals and principles that had become a part of his life. The ultimate ideal for Gandhi, as he repeated several times, is unrealised and unrealisable; its value consists in pointing out the direction. According to him, there must always be an unbridgeable gulf between the ideal and its practice. The ideal will cease to be one if it becomes possible to realise it. He argues: Where would there be room for that constant striving, that ceaseless quest after the ideal that is the basis of all spiritual progress, if mortals could reach the perfect state while still in the body? Striving after the ideal is the very essence of practising Gandhi's philosophy. To the extent we make this effort, to that extent we realise the ideal.

Gandhi's ideals sometimes seem to give a vague impression of the distinction between the ideal and the actual. But he never failed to emphasise the need for his ideals. Gandhi's philosophy lays down moral ideals for individuals and groups to strive for. Their values consist in pointing out the direction, not in their realisation. They cannot be enforced from above but depend upon their voluntary acceptance. The extent to which these ideals can be practised depends on the ethical capacity of individuals or groups. Accordingly, the actual practice of these ideals cannot be uniform. As a social and political reformer, Gandhi spoke from different intensity at different times. But three levels mainly dominate his writings: first, that of the perfect ideal (unrealisable); second, that of his own personal point of view (admitting himself to be far from perfect, yet sufficiently advanced to practise his ideals); third, that of the point of view of the Indian masses. Yet what is implied throughout is this: that even though the ideal may be impossible of attainment, the very act of pursuing it generates the goodwill essential for the well-being of the community life.

The ideal of Non-violent state can never fully be realized. But is there any country that does not want peace, prosperity and tranquility? So, Gandhian thought is a living thought. With the passage of time his thought is becoming more and more relevant with its use of moral principles in each and every walk of life. He realized that it would take a long time for this ideal to be attained. The ideal of Non-violent state of Gandhi, unattainable due to human imperfection indicates the direction rather than the destination, the process rather than the consummation. The Non-violent state will not be an end in itself but one of the means for the achievement of the greatest good of all. It is described as a 'service state' not a 'sovereign state'. Can a state carry on strictly according to the principle of non-violence? Gandhi replied in *Harijan* (September 15, 1946, p. 309), "A government cannot succeed in becoming entirely non-violent because it represents all the people. I do not today conceive of such a golden age. But I do believe in the possibility of a predominantly non-violent society. And I am working for it."

15
Dr. S. Radhakrishnan's Concept of *Sarvamukti*

Dr. S. Radhakrishnan was essentially a self-made man. This life-long philosopher had become the head of a great nation and achieved national and international recognition as 'Philosopher King'. C.E.M. Joad rightly described him as an "heir to a great tradition."[1] The most important aspect of Radhakrishnan's philosophy is that it is a unique expression of an ideal. The very ideal can harmonize the body with the soul, individuals with individuals, and nations with nations. The philosophy of Radhakrishnan is an attempt to reinterpret and reconstruct the *Advaita Vedānta* of Śaṅkara. Great emphasis on the growth of man's spiritual nature is the distinctive contribution of Radhakrishnan's philosophy. In his view body (matter), life, mind (consciousness) and self (self-consciousness) are the manifestations of one underlying, dynamic and creative reality.

Radhakrishnan maintains that man is the highest product of evolutionary process. He accepts that man is determined by his instincts, drives and motives. As a result, he is a biological and psychological individual. But, the real nature of man is his spirituality. He is convinced about the ultimate spirituality of the soul and also the reality of the biological life. Radhakrishnan accepts that there are two aspects of man: physical and the spiritual or the finite and the infinite. Man is a peculiar combination of egoism and self-transcendence. The finite or the biological aspect and the infinite or the spiritual these two aspects are not incompatible with each other. The physical aspect is also equally real and it does not contradict the ultimate spiritual nature. The bodily aspects of man give the evidence of the presence of spirituality and the bodily activities also have a tendency towards self-transcendence. Man has reflection and he can plan his moves. Man has the capacity to live ahead of himself. Radhakrishnan used the word *self-transcendence* to mean this capacity of man.

Radhakrishnan takes full account of the both finite and the infinite aspects of human existence. He explains the finite aspects as those aspects that are determined by the environmental conditions. These aspects of man can be explained by Biology, Psychology and Physiology. Man is a subject living in an environment. Man is essentially subject, not object. The real nature of man is his spirit. The capacity of self-transcendence itself reveals that man is spirit. "Man's inability to achieve perfect contentment in the finite, his unquenchable longing for consummate happiness may be taken as indicative of his supernatural destiny."[2] The human self is described as the latest and highest product of the creative process of emergent evolution in Radhakrishnan's philosophy. The word *spiritual* signifies something higher than the empirical that transcends the subject-object dichotomy. In the domain of Radhakrishnan's philosophy, the import of the word spiritual is explained in terms of self-consciousness. In other words, the spiritual must be of the nature of self-consciousness. "Man is always more than he is able to comprehend of himself."[3]

Human life is integration. Man himself has an aspiration to grow better. His growth is determined by twofold change: the natural change and the spiritual change. The spiritual change is conscious and helped by man himself. He is free to shape his destiny and master the environment. "Becoming better than we were, we realize that we could be better than we are."[4] There is an ever-present urge in man to march towards the realization of spiritual state. "Human development is the development of the spirit in man."[5]

The ultimate human destiny, the goal of man's existence is generally described in Indian philosophy as salvation or liberation (*mokṣa*). The state of liberation which is free from suffering is conceived by Radhakrishnan as the realization of oneness with the reality, world and man from his own metaphysical standpoint. "His (man's) highest destiny is to grow more humane, more spiritual."[6] Radhakrishnan makes suffering and misery of worldly existence an aspect of the process of spiritual growth, but to attain this entirely new state, that of salvation man must be free from the agony, strain and anxiety of the embodied existence. It is not an escape from life, but the purification of one's inner self. It is not the dissolution of the world, but only the disappearance of false outlook. The impulse to perfection is innate in man. The seeking of our highest and inmost self is man's destiny in the true sense. Self-discovery, self-knowledge, self-fulfilment is man's destiny.

Radhakrishnan is impressed by the fascinating concept of *Jīvanmukti* (continuation of the body with liberation). It is a state of living in a condition of *mukti,* while the man is still alive with his body, *Sadehamukti.* "*Jīvanmukti* stands for the highest watermark in human spiritual aspiration and represents the rise of consciousness to new level in man."[7] The liberated individual which is not affected by the world is called *Jīvanmukta.* He works for the good of others in a selfless manner. The *Jīvanmukta* lives and moves in the world for the redemption of others. Being free from egoism and selfishness he dedicates his life and work for the betterment and well-being of the society and of humanity as a whole. It is indicative of a positive attitude towards life. *Jīvanmukti* provides the way of self-transcendence for man. The *Jīvanmukta* wears his life like a light garment.

There is difference between the explanation of the concept *Jīvanmukta* by ancient Indian thinkers and that of Radhakrishnan. "The ancient Indian thinker believes that *Jīvanmukta* becomes *Videhamukta* as soon as he is free from the fetters of the body which as a result of the momentum generated by the forces of the *karma* has continued to exist even after the attainment of *mukti* by the self. But, once this momentum is exhausted the self does not come back to assume any bodily form, he is now fully free from the forces of birth and rebirth."[8] But, Radhakrishnan identifies that when an individual attains salvation with body it does not mean that his task is complete. He has to help others for their salvation. He lives and moves in the world. Therefore, for Radhakrishnan, the liberation of the individual self is not the ultimate destiny of the individuals. The ultimate human destiny is not individual redemption but universal redemption. Radhakrishnan coins the term *Sarvamukti* for universal redemption. C.E.M. Joad has termed it as *social salvation.* It is the final goal of the world-process. "Coherence within the individual and harmony with the environment are both essentials for salvation."[9] Radhakrishnan writes, "For the *Jīvanmukta* obviously the world of plurality, including his own body, does not perish; only he has the right perspective regarding it.....the world of plurality does not disappear, but is lit up by another light."[10]

Generally life is constituted by the instincts, impulses and sensuous contents of the mind. But, man has the capacity to organize, control, regulate and direct the sensibilities. Man's greatness is not in what he is but in what he can be. Radhakrishnan attaches great importance to the fulfilment of his entire being which includes his finite as well as infinite aspects. He is an optimist. Therefore, he holds, "We are living at the dawn of a new era of universal humanity."[11] He has a deep realization of the present-day conditions of man. What the world requires today is spiritual orientation. "The redemption of the human race as a whole is the goal of human history."[12] Radhakrishnan's entire system is based on the ideal of integration within the self and the integration of the self with the Universal self. The well-being of the world in which the man finds himself with his fellow beings is equally relevant to the individual's personal progress.

It is noteworthy that there are certain affinities between the views of Radhakrishnan and modern existentialists. Both Radhakrishnan and existentialists emphasize the potentials of man and present-day condition of humanity. Human destiny for Radhakrishnan is freedom. On the other hand, freedom is a central concept of the existentialists. Though existentialism presents a gloomy picture of life, in spite of present crisis of mankind Radhakrishnan's philosophy bears an optimistic outlook. Radhakrishnan feels that present-day man becomes restless day by day. The benefits of science help man to attain comforts, but he is developing a peculiar uneasiness. As a result, lives both individual and social have become mechanical. In this situation, Radhakrishnan realizes that man exists in the world for a higher cause something more than the earthly existence. Man has an aspiration to grow better. This is the real function to be fulfilled by man himself.

In the midst of recent economic, social, technological developments, it is being forgotten that there is a spiritual spark inherent in every human being. Radhakrishnan's life itself bears the message of peace, harmony, goodwill and faith in the oneness of humanity. He has embodied the spirit of a new humanism and filled us with courage and hope for the future that we should not forget that Indian philosophy always sets before human beings a welfare state.

The Hindu thinkers proposed a truly juristic view of life. "To us the most striking feature of ancient Indian civilization is its humanity. Our second general impression of ancient India is that her people enjoyed life, passionately delighting both in the things of the senses and the things of the spirit."[13] Therefore, the task of man is not to search for his ultimate destiny outside, but to move into himself.

Notes

1. Joad, C.E.M., 1933. *Counter Attacks from the East.* London: George Allen & Unwin, p. 37.
2. Schilpp, P.A., (ed.) 1952. *The Philosophy of Sarvepalli Radhakrishnan.* New York: Tudor Publishing Company, p. 42.
3. Radhakrishnan, S., 1956. *The Recovery of Faith.* London: George Allen & Unwin, p. 87.
4. Radhakrishnan, S., 1959. *Religion and Society.* London: George Allen & Unwin, p. 211.
5. Radhakrishnan, S., 1975. *The Creative Life.* New Delhi: Orient Paperbacks, p. 49.
6. Radhakrishnan, S., *The Recovery of Faith,* p. 7.
7. Rao, Ramakrishna V., 1987. *Selected Doctrines from Indian Philosophy,* New Delhi: Mittal Publications, p. 96.
8. Lal, B.K., 1989. *Contemporary Indian Philosophy.* Delhi: Motilal Banarasidass p. 284.
9. Radhakrishnan, S., 1932. *An Idealist View of Life.* New York: MacMillan & Co., p. 307.
10. Radhakrishnan, S., 1948. *Indian Philosophy,* Vol. II. London: George Allen & Unwin, p. 584.
11. Radhakrishnan, S., 1955. *East and West: Some Reflections.* New York: Harper Brothers, pp. 130-131.
12. Radhakrishnan, S., *The Creative Life,* p. 71.
13. Basham, A.L., 1954. *The Wonder That was India.* New York: George Press, p. 9.

16
Social Reconstruction and the Religious Faith of Sri Śaṅkaradeva

Society is a platform that gives a shape to the people's livings, demands, aspirations, needs and all kinds of growths. But, it is a normal process that time and again society is shaken to the core by different unhealthy elements and factors. In such hour, society or social system should be reconstructed. It is felt that social reconstruction is needed because the traditional system and structures seem incapable to contend with present social problems. Sri Śaṅkaradeva (1449-1568), the great medieval Vaiṣṇava saint of Assam was one who had introduced such a process of social reconstruct 7th centuries ago. His supreme personality had revolutionized Assamese society and culture. The spiritual message of *bhakti* movement of Śaṅkaradeva simplified religion accessible for the most ignorant and the humblest. His spiritualistic humanism tried to wipe off the prevailing social evils of his time. He rejected the cultic rituals and preached in its place a religion of love and adoration. His religious system of *eka-śaraṇa nāma dharma* (the religion of worshipping the One by uttering his name) itself was a successful tool to reconstruct the then Assamese society.

Social Reconstruction

Social reconstruction implies the fulfilment of man's material needs, creative aspirations and spiritual urges. It also indicates social justice. The concept of social reconstruction assumes that our present society is unhealthy or its very survival is threatened by many problems. If society fails to detect that its problem solving strategies and institutions are not functioning well then these become threat to its survival. Social reconstruction assumes that something can be done to keep society from destroying itself. A particular vision of a society is developed which is thought to be better than the existing one and in which problems and conflicts would have been reduced.

Talking about social reconstruction in a civic society very often is based on the supposition that we are in a period of social disintegration. In social reconstruction, it is to discover a social order in which the totality of human interests may find expression. At first a social consensus must be created to reject the faults of the existing society and to affirm the virtues of a future good society. By and large the social reconstruction orientation begins with analysis of society, moves to the creation of a vision of a future good society, and then moves back to handling of the existing social reality to transform it into the future good society. This will provide its members with the maximum possible social, cultural, economic and political equality, satisfaction and justice. In the process, if new social problems and cries would arise, the members of society would also become empowered to continually reconstruct themselves and society. Social reconstruction means rebuilding society. Reconstruction is at the heart of any social work. Social reconstruction can be termed as social reform or self-purification.

Social Reconstruction and Sri Śaṅkaradeva's Contribution

Śaṅkaradeva brought the massage of the *bhakti* faith to every door. His religion entered into the day to day life of Assamese people. All literary and cultural contributions of Śaṅkaradeva were tools to spread the spiritual massage of *bhakti* movement among the masses. Śaṅkaradeva tried to wipe off the prevailing social and other evils that were current in the then Assamese society in the name of religion. He combined religion with art, literature, mass education and social service.

Śaṅkaradeva tried to strengthen spiritual and moral aspects of common individual. Social reconstruction in his philosophy means dual revolution—revolution in the minds of man and revolution in the structure of society. He introduced his *Ek śaraṇa Nāmdharma* when the very concept of religion had lost its spirit. His religion has no caste, creed and colour bounds. Rather, there is a universal appeal to each and every individual of each and every category. Dr. Maheswar

Neog, the eminent scholar of Assam appropriately said that the movement of Śaṅkaradeva promoted a healthy social behaviour and organized a new social build-up.

Śaṅkaradeva established a new democratic social order in the society with the *nāmghara* at the base and the *satra* at the top."[1] The *satras* and *nāmgharas* served as community centres, where people might assemble for community devotional performances like music and drama. *Nāmghara* functions as a prayer hall, a cultural centre, a library and a venue of social assemblage. "*Nāmghara* combined the functions of a village parliament, a village court, a village school and a village church."[2] These institutions took the responsibility of maintaining healthy social relation among the villagers. Consequently, the spirit of co-operation was developed among common villagers. Śaṅkaradeva felt that education is one of the powerful medium of social change and reconstruction. The *satra* also contributed significantly to encourage education.

Śaṅkaradeva declared spiritual equality of all men and denounced caste system. The 'four substances' of Vaiṣṇavism was a great blow to the evils of caste system. In Śaṅkaradeva's Vaiṣṇavism a devotee can transcend the barriers of three *guṇas* in a single life. Criminals, lower class individuals and even nasty spirits can attain liberation if they devote themselves to Lord Kṛṣṇa. Śaṅkaradeva's religion was replete with all comprehended aspects of a healthy religion. He made common people realize that human life had a spiritual fringe.

Śaṅkaradeva's *bhaktivāda* is essentially philanthropic. All *jīvas* are equal, all creations reflect divinity. Equality and equanimity towards all creatures are other significant aspects of Śaṅkaradeva's *bhakti* movement.

Kukura śṛgāla gardhabharo ātmārām
jāniyā savāko pari karibā praṇāma.[3]

(Lord is not only the soul of mankind; He is also the soul of dogs, foxes, donkeys. Knowing this, salute them all.) This character embodies a strong prohibition towards crime and injustice. Śaṅkaradeva's *bhakti* movement proved to be a strong device for a social reconstruction and regeneration.

Equality and equanimity towards all creatures are other significant aspects of Śaṅkaradeva's *bhakti* movement. In the spiritual realm all are equal and everyone has the right to devotion. Fellow-feeling would not possible without spiritual elevation. Sincere urge to get communion with God inspires each individual to love mankind. In this way, *bhakti* leads to humanism. His *bhakti* movement taught lessons on equality, tolerance, fraternity, non-violence and so on, and spread the message of social harmony. In his verses, Śaṅkaradeva spelled out the list of tribes inhabited in different parts of Assam. The motto is to harmonize them and tied them with the thread of *Eka-śaraṇa*. Śaṅkaradeva's mission was to implant altruistic attitude in the mind of common people. So, he declared *Sakalo prāṇika dekhibeka ātmasama*[4] (Regard all beings as your own self). Such attitude is relevant to human society irrespective of ancient or modern century. Śaṅkaradeva's works are full of religious, spiritual and ethical instructions for practising self-discipline.

The realization of the identity of the individual self with the universal self means the identification of oneself with the whole of humanity. Individual soul is a part and parcel of universal soul. Apart from the whole, the individual's existence is inconceivable. The road to salvation lies through love of humanity. It indirectly means freedom from social evils and identification of oneself with everything that lives.

Śaṅkaradeva's doctrine of *bhakti* is simple, liberal and humanistic. He gifted a pure spiritual life to the common people. It is total destruction of egoism. The socio-cultural and spiritual revolution brought by Śaṅkaradeva through his *bhakti* faith caused a huge social elevation by fighting against anti-social elements. His *bhakti* faith leads to spiritualistic humanism.

Music and drama were used by Śaṅkaradeva as two strong tools to educate people spiritually. He was the spiritual torch bearer. He realized that the development of society depended on the education of people and that education should be obviously spiritual education. Śaṅkaradeva wanted to mould the character of common people. His aim was to educate the ignorant using different popular means of communication like music, play, drama, verses and literature.

Śaṅkaradeva's hard struggle for an integrated society made him the greatest socio-cultural spokesman of mediaeval Assam. "On a passage of gloom Śaṅkaradeva's message shone like the brilliance of a mid-day Sun..."[5] Śaṅkaradeva, who brought a social renaissance in Assam, had sown the seed of democracy six hundred years ago. His religious faith exercised a strong and healthy influence on the moral, philosophical and socio-political outlook of the common people.

Śaṅkaradeva enriched the entire cultural life of Assamese people. Dr. Maheswar Neog, the eminent scholar of Assam writes, "The movement of Śaṅkaradeva brought about a new deep and comprehensive outlook of life promoted a healthy social behaviour, organized a new social build-up, fertilized the production of a new *bhakti* based literature in the language of the people and developed a taste for fine arts like music and painting."[6]

B.K. Barua thought highly of Śaṅkaradeva's contribution and expressed that with an all-embracing faith he became a cementing force in such an age when Assam had been politically divided and culturally muddled. Barua maintained that Śaṅkaradeva carved out a way for the cultural, spiritual and linguistic growth of Assam. Śaṅkaradeva wanted to wipe out all prejudices of caste, creed and rank. Śaṅkaradeva made his religious ideas straightforward to such an extent that even the ignorant and humble could join his faith of *Eka-śaraṇa.*

"The only real revolution is in the enlightenment of the mind and the improvement of character, the only real emancipation is individual, and the only real revolutionaries are philosophers and saints."[7] The inner meaning of this statement is suitably applicable in the case of Sri Śaṅkaradeva. The great disciple of Śaṅkaradeva, Mādhavadeva, rightly expresses in his verses,

Srimanta Śaṅkara Hari bhakatara
Janā jena kalpataru
Tāhānta bināi nāhi nāhi nāhi
Āmāra paroma Guru

Srimanta Śaṅkara is, as it were, the tree that fulfils all kinds of desire (*Kalpa-taru*—wish-yielding tree) of the devotees of *Hari.* Verily, verily do I say I have no other great *guru* than Sri Śaṅkaradeva.

K.N. Prasad 'Magadha', renowned Vaiṣṇavite scholar, puts his comments that Śaṅkaradeva's faith "live and let live" had acted positively in shaping the moral and social standard of Assamese life. As Śaṅkaradeva brought a socio-cultural and spiritual revolution in Assam, we should consider his contributions as invaluable treasure and cultural and spiritual inheritance.

Notes

1. Sarma, S.N., "The Satra institution of Assam." In *Śaṅkaradeva Studies in Culture*, p. 83.
2. Kakati, B., A New Life, Letters and a State. In *Śaṅkaradeva Studies in Culture,* p. 14.
3. Sri Śaṅkaradeva, *The Kīrttana. Sri Kṛṣṇar Baikuntha Prayāṇa,* Verse 1821.
4. Sri Śaṅkaradeva, *The Kīrttana. Prahlāda Caritra,* Verse 340.
5. Murthy, H.V. Srinivas, The Lasting Values of Śaṅkaradeva's Teaching. In *Śaṅkaradeva Studies in Culture,* p. 37.
6. Neog, M., Śaṅkaradeva and the Vaiṣṇava Movement in Assam. In *Social Content of Indian Religious Reform Movements* by S.P. Sen (ed.).
7. Durant, W. and Durant, A., *The Lessons of History*, p. 72.

17

Notions of Social Philosophy and their Reflections on Dr. Bhupen Hazarika's Songs

In the informal sense, philosophy is a way of life. But in the formal sense, philosophy is an academic study of different fields. Primarily, there are three major fields of Philosophy—Metaphysics, Epistemology and Axiology. The third field is related to values—Truth, Good, Beauty, Holy, after all the norms. It is a normative field. The discipline Social philosophy is included within this field. Most commonly, as Gisbert put, social philosophy is defined as the meeting point of sociology and philosophy. Social philosophy evaluates the different aspects of man's social life.

Asam Ratna Bhupen Hazarika (1926-2011), an artist of multi-faceted talents was an epoch-making singer who has depicted pieces of bright pictures of love, nature, man, country and nation in his songs. Moreover, highlighting harmony and revolution, he has created a good number of socially significant songs and brought a radical change to the society. His active socio-political life was full of spirit and as a result we have got many evergreen songs as wonderful gifts.

Being social animal, man always lives his life in collaboration and co-operation with other man. The ontological function of social philosophy deals with the fundamental concepts of social life such as man, society, justice, unity etc. Different notions which consist the scope of social philosophy can be summarized as follows: Common good, Social groups, Social ideal, Social consciousness, Social responsibility, Social evils, Social evolution, Social ethos, Social progress and so on. This cataloguing cannot be considered as comprehensive; because, Social philosophy is as dynamic as the social nature or social self of man. Social philosophy provides us with a perspective for problems and issues of society. It takes into account specific cravings of men living in a society. Man's social nature, the relation between individual and society, common good and the relation between common good and the individual good are the subject matter of social philosophy. It also takes different social groups and institutions under consideration. Moreover, Social philosophy enquires into the nature of social ideals and evaluates different aspects of social life in reference to these ideals. Such social values make human life meaningful. Furthermore, there are many diseases of society in terms of social evils. Social philosophy has to deal with the social maladies and the various conditions that lead to such evils. It is the duty of social philosophy to point out how these social evils can be wiped out. Social ethos, culture, social harmony, resolution of social conflicts, social progress etc. are some worth mentioning notions which have been taken care of by social philosophy.

The incredible combination of words, tune and voice made Bhupen Hazarika only one of this kind. He was sincere enough to use his songs as an instrument for social change. He himself said, "If I can do something for society through music, I will hold this life of mine to be successful."[1] Bhupen Hazarika wrote his first song in 1937 at the age of eleven. In this song he acknowledged the priceless contribution of Sri Śaṅkaradeva. We get a glimpse of Hazarika's respect for own society, cultural tradition in this song. The very concept of socio-religious reformation of Sri Śaṅkaradeva found deep rooted in Bhupen Hazarika's life. Though he was a young person at that time, social consciousness of Bhupen Hazarika was really laudable. The spirit of social reformist was honestly expressed in his second song *Agni Jugar Firingati Moi*—Of the fiery age, I am a spark (1939). This song still remains loaded with a sense of revolt. At the same time, from the standpoint of social philosophy, it announces the essence of social change. This song ascertains the rights, freedom and justices to the poor exploited working people. In this song, poet-singer Bhupen Hazarika is determined to manufacture a unique weapon from human skeletons (*narakaṅkāla*) to destroy the exploiters.

Narakaṅkālar Astra Xāji loi
Shosankārik badhim
Xarbahārār Xarbasva punara firāi ānim
(Making arms of human bones
The exploiters I will kill
To the have-nots I will bring back
Whatever they have lost.)"[2]

It echoes the famous declaration of John Locke that whenever any form of government becomes destructive of the human rights of the governed, it is the right of the people to alter or abolish it and institute a new government. The extraordinary weapon of human skeletons (*narakaṅkāla*) symbolizes the empowerment of the oppressed people.

From the very early age of his life, Bhupen Hazarika has been influenced by Jyoti Prasad Agarwala and Bishnu Rabha. Afterwards in his life of America, he has been immensely influenced by Poul Robson. He himself confesses, "Like Jyoti Prasad and Bishnu *Kokāideu* (i.e. elder brother), he was responsible for moulding my philosophy of action. I too wanted to be a singer with the power to change society."[3] Bhupen Hazarika, the soulful wanderer (*Jājābor*) considers inhumanities, injustice, oppression, exploitation etc. as social evils. Moreover, he does not treat such evils of his own country or state as isolated issues. His approach is not individualistic. He even tries to inculcate a sense of universal brotherhood to wage war against such evils. Bhupen Hazarika projects common mass as power. Primary subjects of some significant songs of Bhupen Hazarika are man and society. The song *Mānuhe Mānuhar Bābe* (If humans do not care) is Bhupen Hazarika's stunning success to instil fellow feelings and human love in the hearts of man. He urges people to extend their helping hands to the weaker section of the society...

"Durbal Mānuhe Jodi
Jiwanar Kobāl Nadi
Pār Hoi Tomāre Xāhot
Tumi Heruwābāno Ki
(If any weakling fords
The ragging torrents of life
Clinging to your pluck
What will you lose? Say o mate!)[4]

Following Marx, Bhupen Hazarika announces in his songs that political justice is meaningless without economic justice. He has depicted the miserable life of the poor, oppressed, dominated working class in his songs as universal one. Their pain or distress is not restricted to any race, religion, community and nation or country. The individual in his song is a symbolic spokesperson of a particular class. So, for Bhupen Hazarika *Falahin* on the bank of Nile, *John* on the bank of Mississippi and *Rangmon* on the bank of *Luit* of Assam are identified as one oppressed individual. Bhupen Hazarika's sense of social responsibility is very much potent. He himself has taken the great task on his shoulder to establish the dignity and nobility of the depressed class. His sweet and bold lyrics are for their freedom in a good number of songs.

> *"Xamāyar Xāhere*
> *Likhi Jām Āji Moi*
> *MānuharMukutir Kathā"*
> (I will write, with the courage born of our times
> Of the emancipation of man.)[5]

Bhupen Hazarika's outlook of man is always in terms of society. His social consciousness is so strong that he dares to declare…

> *"Moi Dekhischo Anek Gagonchumbi Attālikār Shāri*
> *Tār Chātei Dekhiso Katanā Grihahin Nara Nāri*
> *Āru Dekhicho Marahā Phular Pāpori Akālate Parā Xari*
> *Bahu Deshe Deshe Grihadāx Dekhi Chintita Hau Bar..."*
> (I have seen rows of colossal skyscrapers
> I have seen lots of tramps under their shades
> I have seen mansions adorned with gardens in the front
> I have seen petals of drooping flowers falling off early
> Having seen menials in so many lands I am worried really.)[6]

Bhupen Hazarika is fluent enough to express his anguish at the hatred and violence in society through his songs. Every time he keeps in his mind an honest desire to guide the society towards love and brotherhood. His songs, on one hand, express fury for the exploiter and on the other hand, a sympathetic feeling for the exploited. A major concern of Bhupen Hazarika's song is the uplift of the working class.

Āh, Āh, Olāi Āh
Xajāg Janatā
Āh, Āh, Olāi Āh, Pohar Ānotā
Rāmare Deshate Thakā Rāwan Badhote
Jāi Jodi Jāi Jibanto Jāk!
Āh Kolā Kākati Faring Nāshogoi Āh
(Come, come, come on out
You the militant masses
Come, come on out
The harbingers of light
If life be spent in slaying Rāvaṇa
In this true land of Rāma
So what if life be spent.)[7]

Bhupen Hazarika is aware of social injustice due to the conflict of rich and poor, exploiter and exploited. But, at the same time, he is bold enough to declare that some age-old social customs and rituals are also to blame for pervading inequality in society. Rituals and restrictions set on the basis of caste and race are also equally responsible. Social progress will not be possible if we stick to unrealistic taboos of society in the name of tradition. In spite of his respect for social norms, Bhupen Hazarika is alert to eradicate such unhealthy customs. His protest in this context is expressed...

"Xarudoi Āideor Ki Hol?
Ki Hol?
Xarukanat Bahibar Man Gol
Lethā Hol
Xamājeo Anumati Nidile
Duyure Jāt-pat Nimile
Xarudoi Xarukane Bijuleer Pohorot
Xaru Xaru Xamājak Ere"
(What has happened to lady Sarudoi?
Yes, what happened?
She desires to marry Sarukan
And it raises a problem.
The society does not allow
As their castes do not match
So, Sarudoi and Sarukan

Leave the bigoted society
In the light of the lightening.)[8]

Bhupen Hazarika propounds secular humanism in his songs. He once said in '*The Sentinel*' the English daily (15th September, 1999), "I have always written and sung songs on problematic themes—whether it has to do with life, society or love." He wants to expand personal love to love of humanity. And finally, it would make social progress smooth. Bhupen Hazarika also speaks of social transition. He is of the opinion that technological advance is also essential for social progress. His dream is always a *Poharar Xamāj* (the society of light) which is a symbolic one. Some songs honestly mirror revolutionary approach to reconstruct society for a new horizon. For example, *Pratitdwani suno moi* (I hear the echo), *Endhār Kātir Nixāte* (In a dark night of November), *Dug Dug Dug Dambaru* (Tom tom tom tom *dambaru*), *Ruddha Karār Duwār Bhāngi* (Forcing prison doors), *Juwati Anāmikā Goswāmi* (Lady Anamika Goswami), *Bhāng Bhāng Xil Bhāng* (Break, break the stones) etc. are the songs which narrate the essence of social philosophy of this genius artist. His deep respect for human values elevates his songs to an incomparable level.

Bajrara Kanthere, Dhumuhār Gatire
Geet Gāi Kapām Diganta
Dānavar Xamājato Gām Mānaware Geet
Kalijār Xasā Xur Xikta
(With the voice of the thunder
With the power of the storm
I'll sing and the horizon I'll shake
In the demon's land, I'll sing
The man's song soaked in hearts true tune.)[9]

Culture makes an individual accomplished. Assamese society is a fabrication of different peoples and cultures. Bhupen Hazarika mentions in his songs different cultural aspects of Assamese society. He sings on cultural and social harmony in the song—*Āmi Asamiyā Nahau Dukhiyā* (Never, never we Assamese are poor). The creations of Bhupen Hazarika, especially poems and songs honestly express the social history of Assam. His songs echo every major socio-political events and movements of Assam. Conflicts, communal riots, inhuman killings, violent acts of activists of different movements, all are resonant in his songs. His association with the *'Bhāratiya Gana Nātya Xangha'* (Indian People Theatre Association) took him close to the common people. At that time he has been enriched with a new spirit of social work for the sake of justice and equality.

> *Mukti kāmi lakksh janor*
> *Mouna Prakāsh Shunisāne Nai*
> (Have you not heard the mute expressions
> Of the freedom loving millions?)[10]

Xudhākantha (nectar voice) Bhupen Hazarika is the artist of the masses. His songs, on one hand, are the result of impulsive and instinctive reaction of his hypersensitive mind and on the other hand, they are his response to the different social issues. Thousands of listeners of his songs become a 'reality' in the metaphysical sense. His social philosophy is truly a realistic philosophy. His songs proclaim that ethical development is the pre-condition of social development—

> *Byakti Jadi Byaktikendrik*
> *Xamasti Jadi Byaktitvarahit*
> *Tene Shithil Xamājak Nābhāngā Kiya*
> (If self seeking are the people
> If spineless is the crowd
> That shaky society why do not you crumble?)[11]

Industrialization and materialism inevitably lead to the concentration of wealth and power in the hands of few rich. This is the root cause of war, violence and conflicts in the society. War and terrorism are throwing their ugly shadow over the world. His songs transmit the mission of remaking the common people with soul-force. His strong nationalism should not be misunderstood as dogmatic one. Though it starts with Assam and Assamese people, ends in world. So, he is rightly said 'world citizen'. His songs always show the supremacy of common individuals. He sings—

> *Itihāshe Siyare Jai Janatāre*
> (History's been clamouring for the people's victory.)[12]

The society Bhupen Hazarika speaks in his songs is not the society of Assam only. It is a one universal society or society in general, so as the norms or ideals of society. His love for human society can be interpreted as comprehensive humanism. His only expectation is—

> *"Jiyāi Thāki Ekhan Xamāj*
> *Garhibar Mor Man Āse,*
> *Jiyāi Thāki Ekhan Xamāj*
> *Garhibar Mor Pan Āse,*
> *Jot Xonatkoio MānuharDām*
> *Alap Haleo Besi Āse*
> (I'll live to raise a society
> It's my ardent wish
> I'll live to raise a society
> It's my fervent pledge
> Where man is worth a little more
> A little more than gold.)[13]

There is hardly any human activity which is not related to man's social environment this or that way. The social life has two sides—the real and the ideal. Society without an ideal will be stagnant and it will not be on the track of development. Social progress always refers to an ideal society as its end. Bhupen Hazarika always speaks of social progress. In his songs common good is embedded moral and spiritual element and that common good makes peace and happiness long lasting. He believes that social evils arise out of the individual's maladjustment to the social ideal.

Bhupen Hazarika's songs express truly philosophical views regarding society and its phenomena. His standpoint has resemblance with that of E. Durkheim. Durkheim also puts forward the thesis that society is a dynamic system and the seat of moral life. In his view, individual is both *I* and *We* (*homo duplex*).[14] Like Durkheim, Bhupen Hazarika is always in favour of an organic relation of the parts to the whole. Three elements constitute the social philosophy of Bhupen Hazarika—inborn social consciousness, truthful understanding of human life and above all a vision for a better future.

Bhupen Hazarika looks social behaviour of man, social events and social institutions in terms of values. His social consciousness got refinement under the guidance of cultural icons of Assam Jyoti-Bishnu. Their socialist ideologies inspired Bhupen Hazarika to a great extent. Very often, Marxists principles and ideas are reflected in his songs. Though his empathy towards the exploited common people is labelled as Marxism, he was not a follower of Marx in the strict academic sense. He bears a secular democratic spirit in him. His social consciousness and responsibility may be called innate. He was intensely stimulated by Paul Robson's words that music is a weapon for social change. His sincere hope is—

> "*Mor Gān Houk Bahu Āsthāhinatār Bipartite*
> *Ek Gabhir Āsthār Gān*
> *Mor Gān Houk, Kalpanā-Bilāxar Bipartite*
> *Ek Xatya Praxhastir Dhyān*"
> (Let my songs be
> A hymn to truth
> Against false imaginings.)[15]

Notes

1. Hazarika, S. (ed.) *Dr. Bhupen Hazarika Rachanawali*, Vol. 1, p. 490.
2. Deka, B. (ed.) *Dr. Bhupen Hazarika: A Legend*, p. 32.
3. Dutta, A.K., *Bhupen Hazarika, The Roving Minstrel,* p. 46.
4. Deka, B., *op. cit.*, p. 132.
5. *Ibid.*, p. 68.
6. *Ibid.*, p. 177.
7. *Ibid.*, p. 152.
8. *Ibid.*, p. 83.
9. *Ibid.*
10. *Ibid.*, p. 259.
11. *Ibid.*, p. 164.
12. *Ibid.*, p. 152.
13. *Ibid.*, p. 148.
14. Durkheim, E., *Sociology and Philosophy.* Translated by D.F. Pocock, p. viii.
15. Deka, B. (ed.), *Dr. Bhupen Hazarika: A Legend*, p. 186.

Bibliography

Agarwal, A.K., 2005. *Role of Alternative Dispute Resolution Methods in Development in Society: Lok Adalat in India*, Research and Publication, IIM Ahmedabad, WP No. 2005-11-01.

Appadurai, A., 1996. *Modernity at Large: Cultural Dimensions of Globalization.* Minneapolis, MN: University of Minnesota Press.

Arizpe, L., Stone, M.P., and Major, D.C., 1994. *Population and Environment: Rethinking the Debate*. Boulder, Colorado: Westview Press.

Basham, A.L., 1954. *The Wonder that was India*. New York: George Press.

Basham, A.L., 2004. *The Wonder that was India*. London: Picador India, Pan Macmillan Ltd.

Bercovitch, J., Kremenyuk, V.A., and Zartman, I.W., 2009. *The Handbook of Conflict Resolution*. London: Sage Publications.

Bharadwaj, K.K., 1993. *Combating Communalism in India: Key to National Integration*. New Delhi: Mittal Publications.

Bhattacharyya, H. (ed.), 1983. *The Cultural Heritage of India*, Vols. III & IV. Calcutta: The Ramakrishna Mission Institute of Culture.

Bhattacharyya, H.M., 1959. *The Principles of Philosophy*. Calcutta: University of Calcutta.

Bloomfield, M., 1972. *Religion of the Vedas: The Ancient Religion of India* (*from Rig-Veda to Upanishads*). Delhi: Indological Book House.

Borkakoti, S.K., 1995. *Sri Sri Śaṅkaradeva—a total Personality*. Guwahati: Bani Mandir.

Borkakoti, S.K., 2006. *Unique Contributions of Srimanta Śaṅkaradeva in Religion and Culture*. Nagaon: Srimanta Śaṅkaradeva Sangha.

Brunton, P., 1939. *Indian Philosophy and Modern Culture*. London: Rider & Co.

Caldecott, L. and Leland, S. (eds.), 1983. *Reclaim the Earth: Women Speak Out for Life on Earth*. London: The Women's Press Ltd.

Chakravarty, B., 2006. *Social and Political Thought of Mahatma Gandhi.* New York: Rutledge Taylor and Francis.

Chaliha, B.P. (ed.), 1990. *Journal of Srimanta Śaṅkaradeva Research Institute*, vol. I, Batadrwa, Nagaon: Srimanta Śaṅkaradeva Gavesana Pratishthana.

Chaliha, B.P. (ed.), 1998. *Śaṅkaradeva—Studies in Culture*. Assam: Srimanta Śaṅkaradeva Sangha.

Chandrababu, B.S. and Thilagavathi, L., 2009. *Women, Her History and Her Struggle for Emancipation*. Chennai: Bharathi Puthakalayam.

Chumakov, A.N., 2010. *Philosophy of Globalization: Selected Articles*. Moscow: Lomonosov Moscow State University, MAX Press.

Crawford, C.S., 1982. *The Evolution of Hindu Ethical Ideals*. University of Hawaii: Asian Studies Programme.

Creel, A.B., 1977. *Dharma in Hindu Ethics*. Calcutta: Firma KLM Private Ltd.

Das, H.K., 2004. *Mahakash Mahasagar Aru Bhupen Hazarika*. Ghaziabad: Mano Publication.

Dasgupta, S., 1994. *Development of Moral Philosophy in India*. New Delhi: Munshiram Manoharlal Publishers Pvt. Ltd.

Dasgupta, S., (ed.), 2004. *The Changing Face of Globalization*. New Delhi: Sage Publications.

Dayal, P., 2006. *Gandhian Theory of Social Reconstruction*. New Delhi: Atlantic Publishers and Distributors.

Deka, B., 2011. *Dr. Bhupen Hazarika—A Legend*. Saurabh Deka, Guwahati: Orchid Publication.

Desai, N. and Thakkar, U., 2001. *Women in Indian Society*. New Delhi: NBT India.

Dev Goswami, R.K. and Mahanta, P.J. (ed.), 1996. *Essays on Śaṅkaradeva*. Beltola, Guwahati: Forum for Śaṅkaradeva Studies.

Devadoss, T.S., 1979. *Hindu Family and Marriage*. Madras: Dr. S Radhakrishnan Institute for Advance Study in Philosophy, University of Madras.

Dhamija, N. and Panda, S.K., 2006. Women empowerment through education. *University News* 44(27). New Delhi: Association of Indian Universities.

Dhawan, G., 1990. *The Political Philosophy of Mahatma Gandhi*. New Delhi: Gandhi Peace Foundation.

Dundes, A. (Ed.), 1965. *The Study of Folklore*. New Jersy: Prentice-Hall.

Dundes, A., 1980. *Interpreting Folklore*. Bloomington: Indiana University Press.

Durant, W. and Durant, A., 1968. *The Lessons of History*. New York: Simon and Schuster.

Durkheim, E., 1965. *Sociology and Philosophy*, translated by D.F. Pockock, London: Cohen and West.

Dutta, A.K., 2002. *Bhupen Hazarika, The Roving Minstrel*. New Delhi: Rupa & Co.

Dutta, D.K., 1982. *Bhupen Hazarikar Geet Aru Jiwan Rotha*. Kolkata: Sribhumi Publication.

Dutta-Barua, H.N. (ed.), 1953. Sri *Śaṅkara Vākyāmṛta*. Nalbari: Dutta Baruah & Co.

Gadkari, J., 1996. *Society and Religion—From Ṛg Veda To Purāṇas*. Bombay: Popular Prakashan.

Glass, B., 1969. *Science and Ethical Values*. Calcutta: Scientific Book Agency.

Gopalan, S., 1979. *Hindu Social Philosophy*. New Delhi: Wiley Eastern Ltd.

Goswami, L., 2009. *Bandita Bhupenda Nindita Bhupen Hazarika*. Guwahati: Aank baak.

Gupta, N.L., 1992. *A Search for Human Values*. New Delhi: Arya Book Depot.

Gupta, S.N., 1978. *The Indian Conception of Values*. New Delhi: Manohar Book Service.

Halbfass, W., 1991. *Tradition and Reflection: Exploration in Indian Thought*. New York: State University of New York.

Halverson, H.W., 1976. *A Concise Introduction to Philosophy*. New York: Random House.

Hastings, J. (ed.), 1981. *Encyclopedia of Religion and Ethics*. New York: Edinburgh, P. & P. Clark.

Hazarika, S. (ed.), 2008. *Dr. Bhupen Hazarika: Rachanawali*. Vols. I-III. Guwahati: S.H. Educational Trust.

Hiriyanna, M., 1952. *Popular Essays in Indian Philosophy*. Mysore: Kavyalaya Publishers.

Hiriyanna, M., 1975. *Indian Conception of Values*. Mysore: Kavyalaya Publishers.

Joad, C.E.M., 1933. *Counter Attacks from the East*. London: George Allen & Unwin Ltd.

Kalita, P., Jalan, G. and Parasar, A., 2007. *Biswanagarik Bhupen Hazarika*. Guwahati: Chandra Prakashan.

Kane, P.V., 1968. *History of Dharma Śāstra*. Vol.1. Poona: Bhandarkar Oriental Research Institute.

Kar, B., 2000. *Value Perspective in Indian Philosophy*. New Delhi: Mittal Publications.

Khan, B., 1965. *The Concept of Dharma in Vālmīki Rāmāyaṇa*. New Delhi: Munshi Ram Manohar Lal Publishers.

Koller, J.M., 1968. Puruṣārthas as Human aims. *Philosophy East and West*. Vol. 18(4) (Oct.). University of Hawai Press Stable URL: http://www.jstor.org/ stable/ 1398408

Krishnamurti, J., 1981. *Education and the Significance of Life*. New York: Harper & Row, Paperback edition.

Kumar, H. and Varghese, J., 2005. *Women's Empowerment, Issues, Challenges and Strategies—A Source Book*. New Delhi: Regency Publication.

Lal, B.K., 1989. *Contemporary Indian Philosophy*. Delhi: Motilal Banarasidass.

MacDonell, A.A., 2002. *Vedic Mythology*. Delhi: Motilal Banarsidass Publishers.

Mahadevan, T.M.P., 1960. *Outlines of Hinduism*. Bombay: Chatana Ltd.

Mahadevan, T.M.P., 1967. Social, Ethical and Spiritual Values in Indian Philosophy. In: *The Indian Mind: Essentials of Indian Philosophy and Culture*. C.A. Moore (ed.) Honolulu: East-West Center Press.

Mahanta, C.K., 1990. The *Kīrttana Sri Sri Sankardeva* (Eng. Translation). Jorhat: Asom Satra Sangha.

Malakar, R., (ed.), 1977. *Teachings of Sri Śaṅkaradeva*. Chandigarh: Sankara Jyoti Association.

Malla, N., 1998. *Nationalism, Regionalism and Philosophy of National Integration*. New Delhi: Regency Publications.

Marshall, A., 1992. *Principles of Economics*. London and New York: Rutledge Publications.

Matilal, B.K., 1989. *Moral Dilemmas in the Mahābhārata*, Delhi: IIAS, Motilal Banarasidass Publishers.

Mazumdar, M. (ed.), 2005. *Encyclopedia of Gender Equality through Women Empowerment*. Vol.1, New Delhi: Sarup & Sons.

Mies, M., 1986. *Patriarchy and Accumulation on a World Scale*. London: Zed Books.

Mies, M. and Shiva, V., 1993. *Ecofeminism*, Halifax, Nova Scotia: Fernwood Publications.

Mondal, S.R., 2012. Interrogating Globalization and Culture in Anthropological perspective—The Indian Experience. *Journal of Globalization Studies*. Vol. 3, No. 1, May Volgograd, Russia: Uchitel Publishing House, pp. 152-160.

Moore, C.A. (ed.), 1967. *The Indian Mind: Essentials of Indian Philosophy and Culture*. Honolulu: University of Hawaii Press.

Mukherjee, R.K., 1950. *The Dynamics of Morals—A Socio-Psychological Theory of Ethics*. London: MacMillan & Co. Ltd.

Mukherjee, R.K., 1965. *The Social Structure of Values*. New Delhi: S. Chand & Co.

Narang, S. (ed.), 1988. *Dharmaśāstra in Contemporary Times*. Delhi: Nag Publishers.

Neog, D., 1963. *Jagat Guru Śaṅkaradeva—The Founder of Mahāpuruṣism*. Nagão, Assam: Sreemanta Sankar Mission.

Neog, M., 1998. *Śaṅkaradeva and His Times—Early History of the Vaiṣṇava Faith and Movement in Assam*. Guwahati: Lawyer's Book Stall.

Olivelle, P. (ed.), 2009. *Dharma Studies in its Semantic, Cultural and Religious History*. Delhi: Motilal Banarasidass Publishers.

Parashar, A. (ed.), 2011. *Mrityunjoyee Duronta Tarun Bhupen Hazarika*. Guwahati: Saaraswat.

Parel, A.J. (ed.), 1997. *Gandhi: Hind Swaraj and Other Writings*. New Delhi: Foundation Books,

Patil, V.T. (ed.). 1989. *Studies on Gandhi*. New Delhi: Sterling Publishers Private Ltd.

Patrick, G.T.W., 2010. *The Psychology of Social Reconstruction*. Charleston SC, United States: Nabu Press.

Patrick, G.T.W. & Chapman F.M., 1961. *Introduction to Philosophy*. George Allen & Unwin Ltd.

Paul, J., 2006. *Globalism, Nationalism, Tribalism*. London: Sage Publications.

Perry, R.B., 2013. *The Approach to Philosophy*. Start Publishing LLC eBook edition.

Plumwood, V., 1993. *Feminism and the Mastery of Nature*. London: Rutledge Publications.

Radhakrishnan, S., 1932. *An Idealist View of Life*. New York: MacMillan Co.

—— 1948. *Indian Philosophy*, Vol. II. London: George Allen & Unwin Ltd.

—— 1955. *East and West: Some Reflections*. New York: Harper & Brothers.

—— 1956. *The Recovery of Faith*. London: George Allen & Unwin Ltd.

—— 1959. *Religion and Society*. London: George Allen & Unwin Ltd.

—— 1975. *The Creative Life*. New Delhi: Orient Paperbacks.

——, & Raju P.T. (ed.), 1995. *The Concept of Man (A Study in Comparative Philosophy)*. New Delhi: Indus.

Rao Ramakrishna, V., 1987. *Selected Doctrines from Indian Philosophy*. Delhi: Mittal Publications.

Reyna, R., 1984. *Dictionary of Oriental Philosophy*. Vol. I, Delhi: Munshiram Manoharlal Publishers.

Ropoport, A., 1974. *Fights, Games and Debate*, Ann Arbor: University of Michigan Press.

Roy, R. (ed.), 1986. *Contemporary Crisis and Gandhi*. Delhi: Discovery Publishing House.

Ruether, R.R., 1975. *New Woman New Earth*. New York: Seabury Press.

Sahay, S., 1998. *Women and Empowerment—Approaches and Strategies*. New Delhi: Discovery Publishing House.

Sarma, S.N., 1999. *The Neo-Vaiṣṇavite Movement and Satra Institutions of Assam*. Guwahati: Lawyer's Book Stall.

Schilpp, P.A. (ed.), 1952. *The Philosophy of Sarvepalli Radhakrishnan*. New York: Tudor Publishing Company.

Sen, S.P. (ed.), 1978. *Social Content of Indian Religious Reform Movements*. Calcutta: Institute of Historical Studies.

Sethi, J.D., 1979. *Gandhian Values and 20th Century Challenges*. New Delhi: Government of India Publication Division.

Shah, B., 2000. Women empowerment in India—the Educational Dimension. *University News*, 38(34). New Delhi: Association of Indian Universities.

Singer, P. (ed.), 1991. *A Companion to Ethics*. Oxford: Blackwell Companions to Philosophy. Blackwell Publishers Ltd.

Singh, A., 2005. Towards women's empowerment. *Indian Philosophical Quarterly*. XXXII (1&2):89-104. Pune University: Department of Philosophy.

Speziale, A., 1987. *The Ethical and Religious Values of Ancient India*. Calcutta: Sujan Publication.

Sztompka, P., 1993. *The Sociology of Social Change*. Wiley Blackwell.

Venkataiah, N., 2007. *Value Education*. New Delhi: APH Publishing.

Visvanathan, N., Duggan, L., Wiegersma, N. and Nisonoff, L. (ed.), 1997. *The Women, Development and Gender Reader*. London: Zed Books.

Warren, K., 1987. Feminism and Ecology: Making Connections. *Environmental Ethics*. 9 (1):3-20. http://www.cep.unt.edu/enethics.html

Warren, K. (ed.), 1997. *Ecofeminism: Women, Culture, Nature*. Bloomington, Indianpolis: Indian Press.

Index